DO YOU KNOW YOUR HINDUISM?

This title is part of a series of books entitled
ESSENTIAL INDIA EDITIONS.
Each book in the series will explore a foundational aspect of the country in new and thought-provoking ways.

ALSO IN THIS SERIES

Our Living Constitution: A Concise Introduction & Commentary
by Shashi Tharoor

Language of the Immortals: A Concise History of Sanskrit
by G. N. Devy

Song of India: A Study of the National Anthem
by Rudrangshu Mukherjee

Dance of Freedom: A Short History of Bharata Natyam
by Leela Samson

The Mysterious World of Tigers: A Book of Discovery
by Valmik Thapar

The Social Life of Indian Trains: A Journey
by Amitava Kumar

A Flag to Live and Die For: A Short History of India's Tricolour
by Navtej Sarna

The Sari Eternal: A Tribute
by Lakshmi Murdeshwar Puri

The Ghosts of Indian Small Towns: A Journey Through Time
by Ruskin Bond

DO YOU KNOW YOUR HINDUISM?

NOTES FOR MODERN-DAY HINDUS

Rajmohan Gandhi

ALEPH

ALEPH

ALEPH BOOK COMPANY
An independent publishing firm
promoted by ***Rupa Publications India***

First published in India in 2026
by Aleph Book Company
161-B/4, Gulmohar House,
Yusuf Sarai Community Centre,
New Delhi 110049

ISBN: 978-93-6523-212-7

1 3 5 7 9 10 8 6 4 2

Printed in India

CONTENTS

INTRODUCTION

Like it or not, with or without our consent, religion is our constant companion. Looming large one moment, it may disappear the next, only to return in another shape or size.

For the great majority of Indians, Hinduism is this constant companion. For non-Hindu Indians, Hinduism is a permanent neighbour.

We walk or run with our religion. Or away from it. At times we rest our weary or troubled minds on it. Or we argue with it.

But there is a big question. Have we really got to know this constant companion or close-by presence? Do we know what Hinduism is?

With Hindus spreading out in every direction, the rest of the world too is curious. This short study is a modest attempt to unveil Hinduism for interested ones today—to present it in a simple and comprehensible manner.

The first and second chapters discuss the principles or values of Hinduism as presented by notable modern Hindus or on occasion by an unknown person. Anyone interested should be able to know what Hinduism stands for.

A major current topic, Hindu nationalism, or Hindutva, as it has been called, appears briefly in the first two chapters and is also indirectly discussed in the third chapter, which addresses the oft-heard notion of Hindus needing to avenge unpleasant history.

The fourth chapter records Hinduism's global expansion in recent years and, among other things, asks if those born to non-Hindu parents can become Hindus. In other words, is Hindu blood necessary for accepting Hindu beliefs and values?

The final chapter, a little one, summarizes the book.

1

WHAT IS A 'HINDU' QUALITY?

My mother's father, a Tamil-speaking Brahmin, possessed an extremely long name, Chakravarti Rajagopalachari. Fortunately, people called him C. R. This chapter is stimulated by a remark that C. R. made long ago, which I will presently quote. First, however, some background.

C. R. lived until he was ninety-four, which was quite an impressive feat in 1972, the year of his death. Even more impressive was the fact that about a quarter century earlier, in June 1948, he had become governor general and, therefore, independent India's numero uno.

In power and popularity, free India's first prime minister, Jawaharlal Nehru, left C. R. far behind. Deputy prime minister Vallabhbhai Patel too carried more influence than C. R. In protocol, however, C. R. firmly outranked both Nehru and Patel.

The Indian who preceded C. R. in occupying the country's highest chair was Bahadur Shah Zafar, the last Mughal emperor. During the ninety years between Zafar's forced exile in 1858 and C. R.'s swearing-in, British viceroys filled that chair.

C. R. had been raised in the 1880s in a poor family in the small town of Hosur, which stood about 40 kilometres southeast of Bengaluru on the same southern plateau, nearly a thousand metres above sea-level. Then part of the princely state of Mysore, Bengaluru would become Karnataka's capital and one of our globe's famous tech cities. Then part of Madras Presidency, Hosur today belongs to northern Tamil Nadu.

C. R. himself rose to become, by turns, a brilliant criminal lawyer; chairman of Salem town's municipality; a prison-going, satyagraha-performing freedom fighter; commander for the

South in Mahatma Gandhi's nonviolent army; premier of Madras Presidency; governor of West Bengal; governor general of India; India's home minister after Patel's death in 1950; chief minister again of Madras Presidency (in 1952), and the founder, in 1959, of the all-India Swatantra Party.

In addition to all of the above, some would say more than all of the above, C. R. was a beloved and hugely popular re-teller of the Mahabharata and Ramayana stories. He also published illuminating commentaries on the Gita, the Upanishads, and the Kural. These religious writings, plus his ability to slide a moral dictum into the political or literary passages his pen was constantly producing, made C. R. one of the last century's liveliest Hindu thinkers.

One evening in the year 1970 or thereabouts, as friends and relatives sat or stood around C. R. in his modest Chennai home, one of his grandchildren spoke of a near one's illness. C. R., who was well past ninety by then, responded by saying, 'Ask Mubarak to pray for her recovery.'

Mubarak was the young driver employed by my mother, who lived a few miles south of her father's home. He was a Labbai, i.e., he had been born into a family of Tamil Nadu's coastal Muslims originating in the eighth century, when traders landing from the Arab world married local women.

After suggesting that Mubarak be asked to pray for the relative who had fallen ill, C. R. added the words to which I alluded at the start of this chapter: 'Muslim faith in God,' he said, 'is undiluted faith.'

Expressions like 'Muslim faith' and 'Christian charity' were common sixty years ago and remain fairly common, indicating that the words 'Christian' and 'Muslim' have also been used as adjectives, and not merely as nouns. Likewise, when we hear of a 'Sikh langar', we know that a meal where no one is left out was meant, not a meal for Sikhs. Here 'Sikh' too is an adjective.

Although on occasion a phrase like 'Hindu stoicism' may be used in general discourse, most of the time 'Hindu' is employed as a noun, not as an adjective. The word is used for an individual or for an organization. Or for another 'thing'. Not for an act. We speak of a Hindu temple, a Hindu locality, a Hindu school, a Hindu political party. Or of the Hindu community. Not generally, of a Hindu *gesture*.

The phrase 'a Parsi cashier' was at times used in Mumbai as an assurance that when you gave the bank a cheque, you got back every rupee. A 'Muslim faith' in God is taken as a faith unaffected by revolutions or disappointments. A 'Christian act' is a charitable or considerate act. A 'Sikh' langar is a meal for everyone. In contrast, 'Hindu' is only occasionally used as an adjective. For the rest of the time, Hindu denotes the race bound up with India that is Bharat, which, however, is no longer a race confined within Bharat's boundaries. This last point is elaborated in chapter four.

Will Hindu values spread worldwide even as Hindu men and women have become global? Will Hindu values become known so widely that the word 'Hindu' gets used as an adjective? Which leads to a basic question. What are Hinduism's principal values?

Before proceeding further on that trail, let us note one well-known Hindu-linked reality in today's world: yoga. It spread worldwide a few decades before the Hindu race conspicuously circled the globe. If today the word 'Hindu' brings to mind something other than a race to people in Europe or Africa, or the Americas, that something, surely, is yoga.

From calming or disciplining the body to disciplining the mind, and disciplining what we speak or write, can be a natural transition. On occasion, a yoga teacher somewhere in the world spells out that connection. Although Hinduism is much more than a yoga session at home or in a gym, yoga is a readymade gateway for Hindu ideas to reach humanity's mind.

What, however, are Hinduism's central ideas? We should recognize that there is no Hindu equivalent for the Bible or the Qur'an. Moreover, there is no historical founder of Hinduism. No originator left a set of Hindu principles. However, we can look at the following presentation, borrowed from the quarterly journal *Hinduism Today,* published from Hawaii.[1]

1. Hindus believe in one, all-pervasive Supreme Being who is both immanent (*inherent in human beings*) and transcendent (*beyond and outside human beings*).

2. Hindus believe in the divinity of the four Vedas, the world's most ancient scripture, and also venerate the Agamas (*ancient verses often connected to Shiva or the Goddess*) as revealed lines. These primordial hymns are God's word and the bedrock of Sanatana Dharma, the 'eternal religion'.

3. Hindus believe that the universe undergoes endless cycles of creation, preservation, and dissolution.

4. Hindus believe in karma, the law of cause and effect, by which each individual creates his own destiny with his or her thoughts, words, and deeds.

5. Hindus believe that the soul reincarnates, evolving through many births until all karmas have been resolved, and moksha, liberation from the cycle of rebirth, is attained.

6. Hindus believe that divine beings exist in unseen worlds and that temple worship, rituals, sacraments, and personal devotionals create a communion with these devas and Gods.

7. Hindus believe that an enlightened master, or satguru, is essential to know the Transcendent Absolute, as are personal discipline, good conduct, purification, pilgrimage, self-inquiry, meditation, and surrender in God.

8. Hindus believe that all life is sacred, to be loved and revered, and, therefore, practise ahimsa, non-injury, in thought, word, and deed.

9. Hindus believe that no religion teaches the only way to salvation above all others, but that all genuine paths are facets of God's Light, deserving tolerance and understanding.

Let me supply an immediate caveat to this 'nine-point summary': Hinduism does not ask for a credal statement from adherents. Reluctance or even refusal to subscribe to some or even all of the nine beliefs mentioned will not make a Hindu a non-Hindu. Non-believers can remain Hindu in their own minds and will so remain in the minds of others in the Hindu community. Ethnicity seems to suffice.

That said, a great many Hindus do believe in *some* of the things listed above. To narrow things down, many Hindus are likely to entertain a belief in some or all of the following: (a) in karma, or the law of cause and effect, which ensures that what we do has consequences, (b) in reincarnation, i.e., the view that a dying person's soul will inhabit some newborn child somewhere, (c) in the value of meditation, (d) in personal discipline and restraint, (e) in surrendering to the Almighty, and (f) in accepting the legitimacy of other religions.

Do Hindus also believe that the whole world is a family? Recent times have witnessed the highlighting of an ancient thought, first spelt out by an unknown Hindu forebear: Vasudhaiva Kutumbakam, or the world is a family. The two Sanskrit words are part of an old verse which can be translated as follows: 'One is a relative, the other a stranger, say the small-minded; to the magnanimous, the entire world is a family.'

While this old Hindu insight is amazingly relevant at this stage of our world's journey, no one should pretend that Hindu parents have been raising their children on that insight, or on the pair of words that summarize it. For one thing, Sanskrit is not a language understood or spoken by 99 per cent of India's population, even though many view it as a sacred language, and even though priests use Sanskrit during marriage or death rituals.

Scholars have told us that the brilliant verse is part of an old text, the Maha Upanishad, which is seen as a subsidiary rather than a principal Upanishad, an Upanishad being any one of several ancient Sanskrit texts that spell out Hinduism's philosophical core.

Hindu children rarely learn the venerated Upanishads, whether principal or subsidiary, or the older, and even more highly venerated, Vedas. Today's Hindu children learn their Hinduism either from religious stories about an ancient past that older relatives may relate to them at home, or—and this is far more likely—they hear the stories on the phone or TV from a modern singer, guru, or activist.

These stories from the past are often but not always centred on the Ramayana and Mahabharata epics or on God Shiva or Siva, his consort Parvati, and their sons Ganesha and Kartikeya, who is also known as Murugan or Subramaniam. Religious festivals that festoon the Hindu calendar and turn up once a month or oftener provide opportunities for entering into the festival's origin and meaning. Hinduism is also conveyed, sustained, reinforced, and often distorted, by TV and social media.

Hindu children or their parents may not have been raised on the Vasudhaiva Kutumbakam phrase, or on the similarly magnificent and equally ancient Tamil expression from southern India, Yaadhum Oore Yaavarum Kelir (Wherever born, he or she is my relative).

Yet it was India's soil that produced the thoughts. This fact can fortify the migrating Indian as also the Indian confined to India's soil. More importantly, the thought should prompt Hindus within India to ask if they think of their land's inhabitants, all of them, as their relatives.

Are we, today's Hindus, focusing on Hinduism's central ideas, including Vasudhaiva Kutumbakam, and demonstrating those ideas wherever we live, whether within or outside India? Are we doing it in ways that enable the world to speak of Hindu deeds, not just of the Hindu race? Will the use of 'Hindu' as an adjective become common? Can the word 'Hinduism' bring to mind a set of these values even before it summons the image of a race, community, or nation?

One of the first Hindus who tried to express Hinduism's core ideas for the modern world was Raja Ram Mohun Roy (1772–1833). Born into a 'high-caste' Brahmin family in Bengal, Roy, who was blessed with curiosity as well as business acumen, engaged with the Mughal empire before it collapsed, and then with the British empire, which replaced it. Learning Persian, Arabic, and English in addition to Bengali and Sanskrit, Roy assisted British officers of the East India Company as one of their 'writers' or clerks from 1803 to 1815.

In 1828, along with Debendranath Tagore (the father of the incredible Rabindranath), Roy founded in Calcutta the reformist organization, the Brahmo Sabha, which proclaimed its opposition to undesirable practices among Hindus such as sati, polygamy, and child marriage. The Sabha also declared its belief, confirmed in the Vedas, in One God for humanity.

Two years later, the titular Mughal emperor, Akbar Shah II, who reigned in Delhi under British sufferance from 1806 to 1837, engaged Roy's services for obtaining an increase in his pension from the British, who had captured Delhi in 1803. This was almost five decades after the Company had replaced Mughal rule in Bengal.

As desired by Akbar Shah, Roy travelled to England, where he succeeded in obtaining a larger pension for his enthroned but needy patron. In 1833, however, Roy died in the city of Bristol, where, nearly 200 years after his death, his memorial continues to draw visitors.

Then there was the already mentioned Rabindranath Tagore (1861–1941). Famed as the first Indian (in fact, the first non-European) to receive the Nobel Prize in Literature, which he obtained in 1913, Rabindranath has left for us an extraordinary legacy of art, literature, music, and wisdom. The contribution to wisdom includes Tagore's ability to clarify for our modern world the meanings of two potent, complex, and connected forces: Hinduism and nationalism.

His book *Gitanjali,* or 'Song Offerings', which was highlighted by the body that gave Tagore the 1913 Nobel, includes this verse of prayer, numbered 36 among the book's 157 poems:

> Strike, strike at the root of penury in my heart.
> Give me the strength to bear lightly my joys and sorrows.
> Give me the strength to make my love fruitful in service.
> Give me the strength never to disown the poor or bend my knee before insolent might.
> Give me the strength to raise my mind

high above daily trifles.
And give me the strength to surrender
my strength to Thy will—with love.

Each sentence in this stanza of six sentences recalls the choice a human being daily faces and expresses a yearning to make the nobler choice. Many in the world of 2026 will readily identify with the sentences, which were written before 1910. If this is the Hindu yearning, then being a Hindu certainly means more than having Indian blood in our veins.

Then there's India's national anthem, written and composed by Tagore, who also produced the song that Bangladesh would adopt as its anthem. Is there another poet whose songs resound from the skies of two nations? Bangladeshis seem to love Tagore's 'Amar Sonar Bangla' as much as we love 'Jana Gana Mana'.

However, only a small number of Indians know that Tagore's original 'Jana Gana Mana' also included the following verses:

Ohoroho Tobo Aahbaano Prachaarito,
Shuni Tabo Udaaro Baani
Hindu Bauddho Shikho Jaino
Parashiko, Musholmaano Christaani
Purabo Pashchimo Aashey,
Tabo Singhaasano Paashey
Premohaaro Hawye Gaanthaa

Jano Gano Oikyo Bidhaayako Jayo Hey,
Bhaarato Bhaagyo Bidhaataa
Jayo Hey, Jayo Hey, Jayo Hey;
Jayo Jayo Jayo, Jayo Hey

Your call is announced continuously, we heed your gracious call
The Hindus, Buddhists, Sikhs, Jains,
Parsis, Muslims, and Christians,
The east and the west come to your throne
And weave the garland of love…

O! You who bring in the unity of the people!
Victory be to You, Dispenser of the destiny of India!

Potono Abhbhudoy Bandhuro Ponthaa,
Jugo Jugo Dhaabito Jaatri
Hey Chiro Saarothi, Tabo Ratha Chakrey
Mukhorito Potho Dino Raatri
Daaruno Biplabo Maajhey,
Tabo Shankhodhwoni Bajey
Sankato Dukkho Traataa

Jano Gano Potho Parichaayako, Jayo Hey
Bhaarato Bhaagyo Bidhaataa
Jayo Hey, Jayo Hey, Jayo Hey,
Jayo Jayo Jayo, Jayo Hey

The way of life is sombre, as it moves through ups and downs
But we, the pilgrims, have followed it through the ages
Oh! Eternal Charioteer, the wheels of your chariot echo day and night on the path
In the midst of fierce revolution, your conch shell sounds
You save us from fear and misery

> O! You who guide the people through
> tortuous paths…
> Victory be to You, dispenser of the
> destiny of India!
> Victory to You, victory to You, victory
> to You…

National Anthems seldom exceed two stanzas. Soldiers may be trained to remain erect, still, and attentive beyond the time that two stanzas take, but national anthems are for civilians too, for children as well as adults. The anthems *must* be brief. The 'Jana Gana Mana' that *we* know is only part of Rabindranath's original song of India, which is even richer and more inclusive than we thought.

We may recognize, moreover, that the Eternal Charioteer whose goodness, wisdom, and victory the song proclaims—visualized in India as the flute-playing Krishna—may be more than a historical person confined by history or geography. He or she may be more than a wondrous child of literature, may perhaps be the timeless Supreme

Being of the universe and everyone in it.

We should look at another defining song that has retained prestige, devotion, and popularity among the world's Hindus: 'Om Jai Jagadish Hare'. Coming after Roy and before Rabindranath, the song's Punjabi author, Shardha Ram 'Phillauri' (1837–1881) was a novelist, historian, poet, and musician born in Phillaur (just north of Ludhiana), whose other works include a biography of Maharaja Ranjit Singh, Punjab's one-eyed ruler who, as long as he lived, foiled British bids to capture Amritsar and Lahore.

Like Roy, Shardha Ram too had learnt Persian. A scholar as well of Sanskrit, Punjabi, Hindi, and music, Shardha Ram wrote a pioneering Hindi novel, *Bhagyawati*, which portrayed women's hardships. Evidently the music of 'Om Jai Jagadish Hare', too, was Shardha Ram's creation.

Although at times rendered as an aarti or ceremonial rite of worship to Vishnu, 'Om Jai

Jagadish Hare' is above all a widely popular song where burdened humans admit their weak condition and turn with complete confidence to an Almighty 'out there' (Paar Brahm Parmeshwar), who is also inside each of us (Antaryaami), for relief, protection, compassion, prosperity.

The short word or sound 'Om' in the following six verses from this song is a sacred syllable representing the universe, consciousness, and the sound of creation.

(1) ॐ जय जगदीश हरे
स्वामी जय जगदीश हरे
भक्त जनों के संकट
दास जनों के संकट
क्षण में दूर करे
ॐ जय जगदीश हरे

Om Jai Jagadish Hare
Swami Jai Jagadish Hare
Bhakt janon ke sankat
Das janon ke sankat
Kshan me door kare
Om Jai Jagadish Hare

Om! Victory to You, Lord of the Universe
Who in an instant removes
Your devotees' crisis
Your servants' crisis
Om, Victory to You, Lord of the Universe

(2) ॐ जय जगदीश हरे
जो ध्यावे फल पावे
दुःख बिन से मन का
स्वामी दुख बिन से मन का
सुख संपत्ति घर आवे
कष्ट मिटे तन का
ॐ जय जगदीश हरे

Om Jai Jagadish Hare
Jo dhyave phal pave
Dukh bin se man ka
Swami dukh bin se man ka
Sukh sampatti ghar ave
Kasht mite tan ka
Om Jai Jagadish Hare

Om! Victory to You, Lord of the Universe
Those meditating on you find the fruit

Their minds are freed from sorrow
Their bodies from pain
Joy and prosperity enter their homes
Om, Victory to You, Lord of the Universe

(3) मात पिता तुम मेरे
शरण गहूं किसकी
स्वामी शरण गहूं किसकी
तुम बिन और ना दूजा
आस करूँ जिसकी
ॐ जय जगदीश हरे

Mata Pita tum mere
Sharan gahun kiski
Tum bin aur na dooja
Aas karoon kiski
Om Jai Jagadish Hare

My Mother and Father Thou
Where else is my refuge?
No one else like you
To bear my trust
Om, Victory to You, Lord of the
Universe

(4) तुम पूरण परमात्मा
तुम अंतर्यामी
स्वामी तुम अंतर्यामी
पार ब्रह्म परमेश्वर
तुम सबके स्वामी
ॐ जय जगदीश हरे

Tum Pooran Parmatma
Tum Antaryami
Paar Brahm Parmeshwar
Tum sabke Swami
Om Jai Jagadish Hare

Most Perfect, Supreme Lord, Art Thou
Knower of my Inmost Being
Controller of the Universe
And everyone's Master
Om, Victory to You, Lord of the Universe

(5) तुम करुणा के सागर
तुम पालन कर्ता
स्वामी तुम पालन कर्ता
मैं मूरख खलकामी
मैं सेवक तुम स्वामी

कृपा करो भर्ता
ॐ जय जगदीश हरे

Tum karuna ke sagar
Tum paalan karta
Main moorakh khal kaami
Main sevak tum Swami
Kripa karo Bharta
Om Jai Jagadish Hare

You are the ocean of compassion
Everyone's nurturer
I, ignorant, chase foolish desires
I'm your servant and you are my Lord,
Shower your grace on me, O Master
Om, Victory to You, Lord of the Universe

(6) ॐ जय जगदीश हरे
दीन बन्धु दुःख हर्ता
ठाकुर तुम मेरे
स्वामी रक्षक तुम मेरे
अपने हाथ उठाओ
अपनी शरण लगाओ
द्वार पड़ा तेरे
ॐ जय जगदीश हरे

Om Jai Jagadish Hare
Deen Bandhu dukh hartaa
Thakur tum mere
Swami Rakshak tum mere
Apne haath uthaao
Apni sharan lagao
Dwaar padaa tere
Om Jai Jagadish hare

Om, Victory to You, Lord of the Universe
You are the friend of the helpless, the remover of sorrows
You are my Lord, O Master, you are my Protector
Stretch your hand
And take me under your protection.
I surrender myself at Your door
Om, Victory to You, Lord of the Universe[2]

This prayer, poem, or song is more than a hymn for Hindus in general. It could be a plea by anyone to everyone's God.

In the year 1998, I picked up on a Delhi three-wheeler a one-page Hindi flyer headlined *Gita-Saar,* or The Gita's Essence. Printed in black-and-white on flimsy paper, the anonymous interpreter's summary of the Gita's teaching gripped me, and I inserted an English translation of the lines into my 1999 study of South Asian history, *Revenge & Reconciliation.* I am delighted to find that this 'essence' can now be seen online.[3] Here, in English, is its message:

> Why do you worry in vain? Whom are you foolishly afraid of? Who can kill you? The soul is not born. Neither can it die.
>
> What has been taken from you that you cry? What did you bring that you have lost? What did you create that has been destroyed? You came empty-handed, and that is how you will go.
>
> Change is the law of the world. One moment, you are the master of millions. The next moment, you have nothing.

> Wipe out mine-thine, high-low, ours-theirs from your mind. Then all belong to you, and you belong to everyone.
>
> This body is not yours; neither do you belong to your body. It is made of fire, water, air, earth, and sky, and there it will vanish. But the soul is firm.
>
> Offer yourself to God, the strongest rock. Whoever recognizes its support is freed forever from fear, anxiety, and grief.

The famous founder of the Arya Samaj, Dayanand Saraswati (1824–83), born Mool Shankar Trivedi in Gujarat's western or 'Saurashtra' region, vigorously contested some of the doctrines of the Sanatani Hindus—the community to which his contemporary Shardha Ram belonged. Winning a large and enduring following in northern India, he is known as Maharshi Dayanand, which means Dayanand, the Great Sage.

Upholding reason, truth, and the status of women, and rejecting idol worship, superstitions, caste distinctions, and untouchability, Dayanand proclaimed the Vedas as the sole textual authority for Hindus. In his appraisal, the Upanishads (which came later), the still-later Puranas, and the Ramayana and Mahabharata epics did not merit unqualified status. Dayanand was as wholehearted as the Sanatanis or anyone else in acknowledging the Supreme Being and in underlining, for individuals, the efficacy of discipline, restraint, and meditation.

Few modern Hindus may be more venerated than Bengal's Ramakrishna Paramhans (1836–86). Often called a worshipper of Goddess Kali, Ramakrishna, born to Khudiram and Chandramani Chattopadhyaya in the Hooghly district of today's West Bengal, had no problem using the word Allah for God, and he was capable also of imagining himself as a Christian.

In the year 1893, Ramakrishna's best-known disciple, Swami Vivekananda (1863–1902), spoke as follows to the Parliament of Religions in Chicago: 'I am proud to belong to a religion which has taught the world both tolerance and universal acceptance. We believe not only in universal toleration, but we accept all religions as true.'[4]

Respect for the other person's religious belief emerges as one of Hinduism's central values, a Hindu quality in other words. This recognition is hugely consequential.

Then there's the willingness to pay a price for the 'good' or the 'honourable' life. In his biography of Netaji Subhas Bose, the scholar Sugata Bose writes that 'suffering' and 'sacrifice', a notion captured by the Hindi or Sanskrit word tyag, was a value 'taught by Ramakrishna and Vivekananda'.[5] Hindus can ask themselves if tyag isn't another value we prize. Wouldn't we want the world to associate tyag with Hinduism?

We honour Netaji Subhas Bose for personifying sacrifice or tyag (or kurbani, a popular synonym for tyag). Not many know that a day before commencing, on 16 August 1945, the fateful flight from Singapore that would take his life, Subhas Bose had ensured a memorial on that city's seafront for the fallen heroes of his Indian National Army that fought for India's independence from Burma, now known as Myanmar.

That Singapore memorial proclaimed the INA's three-word motto: Itmad (faith), Ittefaq (unity), and Kurbani (sacrifice).[6]

Tyag and acceptance seemed to go together in Subhas Bose's life. Acceptance of every compatriot was part of his Hinduism. Inevitably and naturally, his INA had Hindu, Muslim, Sikh, and Christian soldiers and officers.

Isn't acceptance of *people* of other faiths another core Hindu value?

Not much more than a year after Netaji's death, in the months between November 1946 and

March 1947, when Gandhi found himself in the district of Noakhali in the eastern portion of undivided Bengal Presidency, he frequently recalled the Hindu–Muslim partnership that had marked Subhas Bose's Indian National Army.

Independence was around the corner when 1946 turned into 1947, and Partition too seemed likely, but parts of the country, including Calcutta, Noakhali, and Bihar, witnessed Hindu–Muslim violence. In Muslim-majority Noakhali, the victims were Hindus. Imparting courage to them was Gandhi's aim as with a small team he walked relentlessly from one Noakhali village to another, staying in the homes of humble villagers willing to put them up.

A couple of former INA officers were on Gandhi's team. So was his nineteen-year-old grandniece, Manu Gandhi.

In almost every village they entered, Gandhi and his team held public prayer meetings where Hindu and Muslim verses were recited, and prayer songs were sung. At the prayer meeting in Paniala on 22 January 1947, Manu for the first time sang lines which in the years to come would become familiar to millions of Hindus and Muslims: *Ishwar Allah Tere Naam, Sabko Sanmati De Bhagwan* (Ishwar and Allah are both Your names! Bestow good sense on everyone).

Seeing that Paniala's Muslims, who had gathered in large numbers, liked the verse, Gandhi asked Manu where she had picked it up. 'I first heard it in a temple in Porbandar,' replied Manu. 'You should sing it daily from now on,' said Gandhi. Then he added this surmise: 'God Himself breathed it into your mind.'[7]

The rest, as they say, is history. *Ishwar Allah Tere Naam* would resound across India and the world. Hinduism's capacity to accept sounds and words from places on Planet Earth beyond India was again demonstrated.

His life, teachings, and disciples have established Gandhi's close associate, Vinayak Narahar Bhave (1895–1982), popularly known as Vinoba Bhave, as one of the foremost Hindu thinkers of the twentieth century. Born into a 'high-caste' Brahmin community in Maharashtra, Vinoba was, however, more than an intellectual. In the 1950s, he inspired thousands of gifts of land to the landless by walking from village to village in different parts of India and asking landowners to share some of their real estate with the needy.

Another reason for the respect that Vinoba commands is his book on the Gita. Republished many times, the book, a commentary on the Gita's text, is based on talks he gave in 1932 to fellow prisoners serving sentences for defying British rule. In Vinoba's reading, the Gita provides the secret of *equanimity* in this world of sorrows and delights.[8]

In 1940, shortly after the start of World War II, when Gandhi launched a nationwide Individual Satyagraha campaign, he chose Vinoba and

Jawaharlal Nehru, in that order, to be the first and the second among a few thousand individuals across India who would separately and non-violently defy a British law against speaking out. In his journal, *Harijan*, Gandhi explained his selection of Vinoba ahead of anyone else:

'Who is Vinoba Bhave? He is an undergraduate who left college [and] joined the Ashram almost at its inception. In order to better qualify himself, he took one year's leave to prosecute further studies in Sanskrit. And, practically at the same hour at which he had left the Ashram a year before, he walked into it without notice.

He has taken part in every manual activity of the Ashram from scavenging to cooking. Though he has a marvellous memory and is a student by nature, he has devoted the largest part of his time to spinning, in which he has specialized as very few have. Being a born teacher, he has been of the utmost assistance [in developing] a scheme of education through handicrafts....

He has abolished every trace of untouchability from his heart. He believes in communal unity with the same passion that I have. In order to know the best mind of Islam, he gave one year to the study of the Koran in the original. He therefore learnt Arabic. He found this study necessary for cultivating a living contact with the Muslims living in his neighbourhood....

He has an army of disciples and workers who would rise to any sacrifice at his bidding. He is responsible for producing a young man who has dedicated himself to the service of lepers...

He believes in the necessity of the political independence of India. He is an accurate student of history... He has never been in the limelight on the political platform... This will perhaps be the last civil disobedience struggle which I shall have conducted. Naturally, I would want it to be as flawless as it can be.'[9]

If you want the highest standards, start with Vinoba. That, in sum, is what Gandhi was saying.

In March 1948, only six weeks after Gandhi's assassination, forty-seven women and men, who had worked closely with him, met in their late mentor's Sevagram Ashram, not far from Wardha in present-day Maharashtra. Some were seasoned in the political field and others in what was called 'constructive work'.

'What Should We Be Doing Now?' was the question posed for the two-day dialogue.

Prime Minister Nehru was there. So was Vinoba. A heart attack prevented Vallabhbhai Patel from joining. Other participants included Rajendra Prasad, who would become India's first president; Abul Kalam Azad, free India's first education minister; and Jayaprakash Narayan, the nation's hero in the Quit India movement of 1942 and again during the 1975–77 'Emergency'.

Also taking part were fascinating individuals like J. B. Kripalani, who was the Congress president when, in August 1947, India became free and was partitioned; his wife, Sucheta Kripalani;

Rajkumari Amrit Kaur; Bibi Amtus Salam; Mridula Sarabhai; Zakir Husain (another future president of India); J. C. Kumarappa; and others.

All were gifted individuals. The life of each had been carved by courage, dedication, and sacrifice. Those not in politics agreed during this conclave that Vinoba should lead them, while Vinoba said to Nehru, 'We are yours and you are ours. Your difficulties are our difficulties.'[10] There was a sense of family, but also a sense of separate responsibilities.

Vinoba made an important point to this 'family' of the Gandhi-led movement:

'Do we insist on cleaving to the truth merely because Gandhiji says we are to do so? Is truth held in high esteem because of Gandhiji? Or is Gandhiji held in high esteem because of truth? [His] principles did not belong to Gandhiji. They were manifested by him. When I adopt them, they become mine… [T]here is no need to present them in Gandhiji's name.'[11]

Vinoba proceeded, at this conclave, to make

a second point, directly relevant to our understanding of Hindu nationalism. He said:

'I belong to the state where the RSS came into being. Here I am, having relinquished caste, but still I cannot forget that I belong to the caste of the man who committed this act (*the assassination*) … I was silent with sadness. In addition to sadness, I also felt shame….

This organization has been spread far and wide and with great skill, and its roots have struck very deep.'

Adding that the democratic goal and democratic procedures were missing in the RSS, Vinoba pointed out that the RSS had 'made particular usage of the Maharashtrian intellect. In all the states, its leaders and chief organizers have mostly been Maharashtrians, and mostly Brahmins; their Guruji too is a Maharashtrian Brahmin.'

'The members of this organization do not take others into their confidence. Gandhiji's principle was that of truth; it seems to me that the principle of these people must be that of untruth. This untruth is an integral part of their technique and their philosophy.'[12]

Nonetheless, added Vinoba:

'We will not go anywhere by heaping all the blame onto the RSS. They are people who think differently from the way we do. But there are some good, self-sacrificing people to be found among them, deserving of our respect.'[13]

Is Hindu nationalism part of Hinduism? Is nationalism another Hindu value? Or is nationalism a universal, human urge, with constructive as well as divisive implications? Is it not an urge that Buddhists, Christians, Muslims, and Jews, too, may share? This is a question that must be faced in any serious discussion of Hinduism and Hindu values.

It is not my claim that the examples and quotes I have supplied trace in any exact sense the journey of Hindu thinking in the last two hundred and fifty years. However, while the selections are personal, they broadly align, I submit, with history's graph. Moreover, the Hindu thinkers I have cited in defence of tolerance and friendship were only confirming in fresh ways what the unknown sage had intuited a few thousand years ago in the Rig Veda:

Ekam sat vipra bahudha vadanti. (Truth is one. The wise speak of it in many ways.)

(Rig Veda, 1.164.46)

'Hindu', we may conclude, is more than a noun. A Hindu approach to another human being, to *any* other human being, is an approach of acceptance, respect, and goodwill. If adopted by enough men and women born as Hindus, the approach might one day be called by others *the Hindu* approach.

Most Indians starting a new life elsewhere on our planet do not reject the culture of the India they're leaving behind. Given the smartphone, to say they are leaving India behind would be an error anyway.

Unlike migrants in earlier periods who left lands in Eastern Europe or elsewhere for the freedom of belief that North America offered, most Indians moving to the Western ecosphere are embracing a new culture without rejecting the culture they are 'leaving behind'. They are glad and proud to be bicultural.

The depth of the attachment of India's migrating Hindus to the land of India, and, in particular, to the sacred mountains and rivers of Mother India, should be recognized. While hundreds of Hindu temples have been created in 'the Western world', almost always with traditional architecture and the use of traditional stone, it is not that easy to picture the Mississippi River (or the Thames, the Rhine, the Seine, or the Volga) as the Ganga or the Kaveri. Or to idolize the

Rockies the way the Himalayas are venerated.

Nonetheless, reflection, physical distance, and the realities of climate change can sharpen our thinking. How wise was it for us to see India's mountains and rivers as being entirely divine? By making them purely divine, we gave the mountains and the rivers the task of looking after us, when in fact it was our task to look after them, to protect them from the ravages of human throngs, which remain ravages even when pilgrims and worshippers constitute the throngs.

Whether or not the rivers and mountains have cleansed us of our sins, we have certainly dirtied our rivers and our peaks.

And we have hastened the weakening of our greatest asset, the towering Himalayas. We didn't realize that our mountains and rivers, too, were part of a human family we had to take care of.

Something similar may be said about another asset of an entirely different kind that we worship: the Sanskrit language. The intonations of a rhythmic Sanskrit verse transport many of us to another space. They summon the scent of incense, the tinkle of temple bells, the image of ancient ascetics lost in divine contemplation. We impute divinity to the sounds, to a particular way of combining consonants and vowels that exist in our earth's other languages as well.

When a few years ago I first met an American scholar of Sanskrit who had translated *the whole* of Valmiki's Ramayana from Sanskrit to English and shook his hand, for a second or two I felt I was in physical contact not only with a scholar of immense learning, discipline, and dedication, but also, through his hand, with a divine age and maybe with the warmth of divinity itself.

As I analyse that momentary feeling, I find both respect and sentimentality in it. The respect, growing with my perusals of the translation, is more than merited. It is also mingled with amazed gratitude for the devotion by a 'foreigner' of a good chunk of his lifetime to a text precious to people like me.

The sentimental part, however, has receded, and reason has taken over. I ask the obvious questions. Is a Greek or a Latin Bible more divine than one in English or French? An Arabic Qur'an more divine than one in Urdu? A Buddhist text more divine in Pali or Sinhala than in Japanese? Is a Sanskrit Gita divine in a sense that a Hindi or English Gita cannot be?

Such questions, too, may be relevant to our understanding of Hinduism and its core values.

2

MAHATMA GANDHI'S HINDUISM

One of the best-known Hindus of modern times, Mohandas Karamchand Gandhi (1869–1948), the Bapu or father of India's movement for Independence from the British, was an early NRI, or non-resident Indian, who spent three years studying in the UK and twenty years as a lawyer-activist in South Africa before returning 'permanently' to India in 1915. I insert the quotation marks because Gandhi continued to belong to a wider world.

I give a whole chapter in this short book to Gandhi's Hinduism because I have studied Gandhi more than the others, not because I've concluded that other Hindu thinkers are less significant.

'Every fibre of my being is Hindu,' Gandhi would

sometimes say.[14] With that remark he not only identified himself with the Hindu race—with the ethnic community today seen everywhere in the world—he also conveyed his acceptance of key Hindu tenets. However, when Brahmin priests cited ancient verses defending untouchability and child-marriage to him, Gandhi interrupted them, saying:

> The proper way of upholding Hinduism [is] not by quoting isolated texts but by acting through the inner voice of conscience. Nothing that was opposed to truth and love could be dharma.[15]

This was in 1927. Ten years earlier, in November 1917, when defenders of untouchability had thrown old verses to him, Gandhi replied,

> It is no good quoting verses from the Manusmriti and other scriptures in defence.... A number of verses in these scriptures are apocryphal, a number of them are quite meaningless....[16]

He used stronger words for untouchability. He said in Madras on 16 February 1916: 'Every affliction that we labour under in this sacred land is a fit and proper punishment for this great and indelible crime that we are committing.'[17]

In 1918, Gandhi repeated his position that he would ignore or defy a religious practice if it offended 'reason and morality'.[18] Concord with 'reason and morality' may, therefore, be seen as *the first feature* of Gandhi's Hinduism. In 1928, Gandhi gave reasoned (and rhythmic) expression to his faith in God, saying,

> In the midst of death, life persists; in the midst of untruth, truth persists; in the midst of darkness, light persists. Hence, I gather that God is Life, Truth, Light. He is Love. He is the Supreme Good.[19]

Twenty years later, however, in January 1948, Gandhi said he preferred the expression, 'Truth is God' to 'God is Truth'. He made the remark while breaking what would be his life's last fast, which had been undertaken in a season that saw carnage in different parts of India and Pakistan. Gandhi explained his fresh choice of words:

> I embarked on the fast in the name of Truth whose familiar name is God.... In the name of God, we have indulged in lies, massacres of people, without caring whether they were innocent or guilty, men or women, children or infants. We have indulged in abductions, forcible conversions, and we have done all this shamelessly. I am not aware if anybody has done these things in the name of Truth. With that same name on my lips, I have broken the fast.[20]

If Gandhi's Hinduism was rational, it was also accepting of non-Hindus. He rejected any notion of Hindus as India's superior or ruling race or community. In his view, Hindus, Muslims, Christians, and followers of other faiths were entitled to equal rights in India and meant to live in friendship with one another. This was *the second feature* of Gandhi's Hinduism.

Gandhi's rejection of notions of incompatibility between Hindus and Muslims, and his rejection of any difference in their status in India's society or polity, remained lifelong positions. In his *Hind Swaraj*, written in 1909, i.e., nearly four decades before India's independence, Gandhi had said:

> India cannot cease to be one nation because people belonging to different religions live in it. In reality there are as many religions as there are individuals; but those who are conscious of the spirit of nationality do not interfere with one another's religion.
>
> In no part of the world are one nationality and one religion synonymous terms; nor has it ever been so in India....
>
> Is the God of the Muslim different from the God of the Hindu? ... There are deadly proverbs as between the followers

> of Siva and those of Vishnu, yet nobody suggests that these two do not belong to the same nation.[21]

We can see this as Gandhi's theory of Indian nationhood in 1909. It remained his belief until his death in 1948. Hindus, Muslims, and people of other faiths all belonged to India, and there was no question of any gradation of rights between them.

A third aspect of Gandhi's Hinduism was an openness to texts from the rest of the world. No doubt Hinduism was uniquely and intimately bound to India. The second-class status of Indians in their own land during British rule offended Gandhi and incited him to organize all-India movements for independence, making him a 'nationalist'. However, the world was not shut out either by Gandhi's Hinduism or by his nationalism.

This openness was already apparent when, as a nineteen-year-old law student in London,

Gandhi read the Gita there. He had not encountered the Gita earlier. The Ramayana used to be recited in Gandhi's boyhood home in Rajkot. He was familiar with Hindu bhajans and had been moved by the moral stories of Harishchandra, Prahlad, and Shravan. But he had not perused the Gita. Reading it in London, in Edwin Arnold's English-verse rendering, Gandhi was captured. For the rest of his life, Gandhi would speak of Arnold's *Song Celestial* as the Gita's finest translation.

Five years after reading *Song Celestial*, when Gandhi found himself in South Africa, Leo Tolstoy's *The Kingdom of God Is Within You* stirred and influenced him. Focusing in this book on Jesus's Sermon on the Mount, Tolstoy underlined five commandments: love your enemies, and do not hate, lust, hoard, or kill. The twenty-four-year-old Gandhi was 'overwhelmed', he would later say in his *Autobiography*, by the 'independent thinking, profound morality, and truthfulness' in Tolstoy's presentation.[22]

When, in November 1907, Gandhi's journal in South Africa, *Indian Opinion,* invited essays on civil disobedience and announced prizes, it asked essay writers to absorb the writings of Tolstoy, Henry David Thoreau, and the story of Socrates, and to provide 'Biblical and other religious authorities' for their views.[23] This thirty-eight-year-old Indian, a Hindu in every fibre of his being, was interested in the finest thoughts from the rest of the world.

In 1921, six years after returning to India, a fifty-one-year-old Gandhi described the texture of his nationalism in the course of a fascinating debate with Rabindranath Tagore:

> I do not want my house to be walled in on all sides and my windows to be stuffed. I want the culture of all lands to be blown about my house as freely as possible. But I refuse to be blown off my feet by any.[24]

In October 1928, Gandhi wrote:

> I have nothing to be ashamed of if my views on Ahimsa are the result of my Western education. I have never tabooed all Western ideas, nor am I prepared to anathematize everything that comes from the West as inherently evil.[25]

Not that Gandhi was admitting that his ahimsa or nonviolence was of Western origin. In fact, he often cited ahimsa as the supreme duty—paramo dharma—noting its presence in old Hindu texts, including the Mahabharata, as also in ancient Buddhist and Jaina teaching. However, if critics charged that his nonviolence had a 'Christian' or 'Western' origin, Gandhi's response, in effect, was, 'So what?'

About twenty years later, in April 1947, when independence was only four months away, many of Asia's leaders journeyed to Delhi and assembled in the Purana Qila. An Egyptian delegate recalled an Arabic poem that started by recalling the spindle with which, every day, Gandhi made cotton thread:

> The spindle in Gandhi's hand became sharper than the sword,
>
> The simple white sheet wrapping Gandhi's thin body was an armour-plate, which imperial guns could not pierce,
>
> Gandhi's goat became stronger than the British Lion.[26]

Gandhi addressed the leaders of Asia for a few minutes. I was there in the Old Fort as an eleven-year-old and heard him. Said Gandhi:

> All the Asian representatives have come together. Is it in order to wage a war against Europe, against America, or against non-Asians? I say most emphatically, 'No.'[27]

Speaking of Zoroaster, the Buddha, Moses, Jesus, and Muhammad, Gandhi described the five as

'Asia's wise men' and added, 'I do not know of a single person in the world to match these men of Asia.' He went on to say:

> I [am] an inheritor of the message of love that these great unconquerable teachers left for us. I want you to go away with the thought that Asia has to conquer the West through love and truth. In this age of democracy, in this age of awakening of the poorest of the poor, you can redeliver this message with the greatest emphasis.
>
> You will complete the conquest of the West not through vengeance because you have been exploited, but with real understanding.... This conquest will be loved by the West itself.[28]

Another noteworthy aspect of Gandhi's Hinduism, *the fourth* in this survey, was his frank departure from the 'guru-disciple' tradition. He would say he never found a guru who could satisfy him completely, and never felt he had a guru's perfect qualities entitling him to adopt disciples.

Moreover, in Gandhi's Hinduism, God, the ruler of life, death, and the universe—whether addressed as Shiva or Ram or Krishna or something else—was clearly and unmistakably distinct from namesakes in popular mythologies.

On November 18, 1947—two-and-a-half months before his death—Gandhi wrote in a letter:

> My Ram is not a man with two hands and two feet. But if I am perfectly fit, it is due to Ram's grace.[29]

We may note this as *the fifth feature* of Gandhi's Hinduism. The popular refrain associated with Gandhi and addressed to the Almighty, 'Ishwar Allah Tere Naam' (You are Ishwar, you are Allah), was not invented by Gandhi, but his life, message, and legacy are fused with that line.

When I visited Noakhali, in Bangladesh, in November 2000, which was fifty-four years after Gandhi's trek there in the winter of 1946–47,

I asked residents I bumped into on Noakhali's country roads if they remembered Gandhi. They did not know that I was Gandhi's grandson or someone from India.

The reply of a man who gave his name as Sirajul Islam Majumdar of village Kamalpur, a man who seemed to be in his late fifties, the son, as he informed me, of Dr Khaleelur Rahman Majumdar, was as follows:

> My father told us of *Raghupati Raghav Raja Ram, Ishwar Allah Tere Naam.*

Sirajul Islam did not just pronounce these words. He *sang* them. This was fifty-four years after his father had heard the words from Gandhi, and in immediate response to a question he had encountered by accident on a country road. Sirajul Islam then added with some pride, 'My grandfather protected Hindus on his roof during the rioting.' He was speaking of the riots of 1946.

Gandhi wanted Sirajul Islam's father, and everyone else, to be reminded of the ancient human understanding that people use a variety of names to address the same Ruler of the universe. On 27 September 1947, four months before he would die, Gandhi said in Delhi: 'My physician today, in my thought, speech and action, is Ram, Ishwar, Rahim.'[30]

Which meant that his Hinduism did not separate Gandhi from anyone. On 12 November 1947, when Diwali fell, Gandhi said:

> We must kindle the light of love within. Can you, every one of you, lay your hand on your heart and say that every sufferer, whether Hindu, Sikh, or Muslim, is your own brother or sister?[31]

The sixth feature of Gandhi's Hinduism is the place he gives to ahimsa and satyagraha in humankind's struggles. Though exalted in Hindu texts, in practise the ancient doctrine of ahimsa had been reduced to rules of diet until Gandhi turned it into an explosive yet constructive force by linking it to satyagraha.

The word satyagraha, we might mark, is Gandhi's gift to language, while the conscious nonviolent resistance connoted by that word is Gandhi's gift to the modern world.

An elderly Russian I met in Moscow in 1994 told me of what he remembered from the year 1922, i.e., more than seven decades prior to our meeting, which was the impact on Russians of Gandhi's abrupt suspension of an India-wide campaign. Gandhi called it off because an angry crowd had brutally killed twenty-two Indian policemen employed by the British empire. This response of Gandhi, the aged Russian told me, was contrasted in the Moscow of 1922 with Lenin's defence of the murder of some of the 'class enemy' while they lay ill in a hospital. 'These things happen in a revolution,' Lenin had evidently said.

If satyagraha barred cruelty by a mob, it empowered the weak and even the crippled. As *Hind Swaraj* put it in 1909, well before the Russian revolution, 'Even a man weak in body is capable of offering this resistance. One man can offer it just as well as millions. Both men and women can indulge in [it].'[32]

After much of India took part in the satyagraha of 1930, which had begun with the Salt March, Churchill told the House of Commons that Indians had 'inflicted such humiliation and defiance as has not been known since the British first trod the soil of India'.[33]

Violence, on the other hand, inflicted and invited harm on disadvantaged humans, including people on your side. As Gandhi explained in 1931:

> We cannot win Swaraj for our famishing millions, for our deaf and dumb, for our lame and crippled, by the way of the sword.... If the practice of seeking justice through murders is established amongst us, we shall start murdering one another for what we believe to be justice. In a land of crores of destitutes and crippled persons, this will be a terrifying situation.[34]

On Gandhi's theory of nonviolent resistance, let me quote Professor James M. Lawson. In the 1950s and 1960s, Lawson, who died in 2024 at the age of ninety-five, was one of Martin Luther King Jr's closest colleagues. In 2022, Lawson wrote in his book, *Revolutionary Nonviolence*: 'As Albert Einstein is the father of Physics, so is Gandhi of India the father of nonviolence.'[35]

Feature number seven of Gandhi's Hinduism is its identification of male domination as a major human flaw. Gandhi acknowledged the flaw in his own life—in his treatment of his wife, Kastur. In October 1938, while visiting undivided India's North West Frontier Province, this is what Gandhi told an audience of Pashtun males, all keen to defy British rule, in a place called Hangu, about 40 kilometres south of today's Pakistan–Afghanistan border:

> I used to be a tyrant at home.... I used to let loose my anger at Kasturba. But she bore it all meekly and uncomplainingly. I had a notion that it was her duty to obey

me, her lord and master, in everything.... [S]lowly it began to dawn upon me that I had no such prescriptive right over her. If I wanted her obedience, I had first to persuade her by patient argument. She thus became my teacher in non-violence.

I literally used to make life a hell for her. Every other day I would change my residence, prescribe what dress she was to wear. She had been brought up in an orthodox family, where untouchability was observed. Muslims and untouchables used to frequent our house. I made her serve them all, regardless of her innate reluctance.

But she never said 'no'. She was not educated in the usual sense of the term and was simple and unsophisticated. Her guileless simplicity conquered me. You all have wives, mothers and sisters at home. You can take the lesson of non-violence from them.[36]

In these sentences, clearly aimed at macho Pashtuns, Gandhi admits that Kastur became his teacher in nonviolence by questioning him and confronting him with his domineering side. Despite the orthodoxy instilled into her, Kastur accepted his radical steps—as a partner, not as a subordinate.

Finally, we may mark *feature number eight* of Gandhi's Hinduism: his focus on the individual. About two weeks before he was killed, Gandhi told his prayer-meeting audience:

> *14 Jan. 1948*. Society is made up of individuals. It is we that make society.... If one man takes the initiative, others will follow, and one can become many; if there is not even one, there is nothing.[37]

Freedom of the press flowed from individual freedom. When, in 1940, British rulers ordered Gandhi not to report in his journals that his close associate, Vinoba Bhave, had been arrested, Gandhi suspended the journals' publication and wrote:

> Let everyone become his own walking newspaper and carry the good news from mouth to mouth.... [I can] tell my neighbour what I have authentically heard. This no Government can overtake or suppress. It is the cheapest newspaper yet devised and it defies the wit of Government, however clever it may be.
>
> Let these walking newspapers be sure of the news they give. They should not indulge in any idle gossip. They should make sure of the source of information, and they will find that the public gets all the information that they need without opening their morning newspaper...[38]

Was Gandhi anticipating social media? He was certainly underlining the right of free speech, which lay at the heart of his religious belief.

'GANDHI SHOULD HAVE FASTED AGAINST PARTITION'

If Gandhi was opposed to India's division, why didn't he fast against Mountbatten's Partition Plan in the summer of 1947? In 1932, he had fasted in Pune against separate electorates for Dalits. In September 1947, he fasted in Calcutta for Hindu–Muslim peace. In January 1948, he again fasted for communal peace in Delhi. Why then did he not oppose India's division with a fast?

There was a hint of that question in a comment made by the RSS chief, Mohan Bhagwat, on 28 August 2025, when the organization celebrated its hundredth anniversary.

'It is wrong to say that the RSS did not protest against Partition. The Sangh had protested against it, but what power did the Sangh have at the time? The entire nation was following Mahatma Gandhi.'[39]

Natural, reasonable, innocent remarks? You might think so, except that they aren't quite. Especially when you know the facts, which are as follows.

When, in March 1940, Jinnah and the Muslim League first demanded a Pakistan consisting of Muslim-majority parts of India under British rule, Gandhi spelt out half a dozen problems with the idea. Six months later, i.e., in September 1940, he made an emotional remark at a meeting in Bombay of the All-India Congress Committee:

> I do not say this as a Hindu. I say this as a representative of Hindus, Muslims, Parsis, and all. I would say to Muslim brethren, 'Cut me to pieces first and then divide India. You are trying to do something which was not attempted even during the Muslim rule of 200 years. We shall not allow you to do it.'[40]

In saying, '*We* shall not allow you to do it,' Gandhi was speaking for the Indian National Congress (INC), the country's largest and most representative political organization at the time. The INC's president in 1940 was Abul Kalam

Azad. Persons like Nehru, Patel, Rajendra Prasad, Rajagopalachari, Abdul Ghaffar Khan, Sarojini Naidu, Kripalani, and Gobind Ballabh Pant constituted the rest of the leadership, but Gandhi was the acknowledged 'Bapu'. He was the INC's guide.

The picture was entirely different seven years later, in June of 1947, when a new Viceroy, Mountbatten, presented his Partition Plan. Those seven years had seen World War II, the Quit India movement inside India, and the incarceration, for much of that time, of the INC's leadership.

After the War ended and the leaders were released in the summer of 1945, Gandhi, though still called Bapu, was no longer the Congress's decision-maker. That role would hereafter be exercised by Nehru and Patel, working jointly.

By the summer of 1947, Nehru, Patel, and almost all their INC colleagues, including the new party president, Kripalani, were clear about two things. One, the British were finally departing. Even if begged to stay on (which no one was asking them to do), they wouldn't. They had made up their minds to leave. Quit India's goal had been achieved.

The second conclusion reached before the 1947 summer by Patel, Nehru, and their principal colleagues was that the Partition, which they and everyone in the Congress had opposed ever since it was first demanded in 1940, would actually enable them to provide an unimpeded, efficient, and strong government to the subcontinent's Hindu-majority portion, which was three-fourths of the whole.

The 'interim government' installed in September 1946, consisting of Nehru, Patel, and some others from the Congress, and Liaqat Ali Khan and some others from the Muslim League, all subject to the chairmanship of Lord Wavell, the British Viceroy, had been a disaster. Governing three-fourths of India without obstruction from the League was a welcome alternative.

Moreover, a Hindu–Muslim civil war on a subcontinental scale loomed on the horizon. Frightening rehearsals for such a war had already been staged in some places—in Calcutta in August 1946, in East Bengal in September 1946, in Bihar in September–October 1946, in western UP in November 1946, and in West Punjab in March 1947. Elsewhere in the country, Hindu–Muslim relations had been damaged by ill-will, suspicion, and bitterness, in and from both sides.

As the year 1947 advanced, Nehru, Patel, and their colleagues thought that a wider conflagration could be prevented by establishing two separate but cohesive administrations. Patel and Nehru were confident that, at least in its truncated space, the Indian government would ensure peace and goodwill.

In 1947, there was no noticeable opposition to dividing India from non-Congress parties or groups like the RSS. When in the first week of March 1947 riots targeting Sikhs and Hindus occurred in western Punjab, in and around Rawalpindi and Multan, the leaders of Punjab's Hindu and Sikh communities swung their weight firmly in favour of partitioning their province and creating a self-governing Eastern Punjab where the Sikhs and Hindus would outnumber Muslims.

An identical position was taken by influential Hindus in undivided Bengal. From the autumn of 1946, Shyama Prasad Mukherjee of the Hindu Mahasabha had been fighting openly and persuasively for dividing Bengal to produce a Hindu-majority West Bengal.

In 1951, on the RSS's urging, Mukherjee would head a new political party, the Bharatiya Jan Sangh.

A role in the acceptance of Partition was played by V. P. Menon, the talented civil servant who at independence moved from the Viceroy's staff to become Patel's chief officer for integrating the princely states. Just before that, during the months prior to independence, and this is scarcely remembered today, Menon was the intermediary between India's British rulers and Patel, whose confidence he had won.

In Menon's 1957 book, *Transfer of Power,* we are given an eyewitness account of Patel's conversion, at the end of December 1946, to the idea of Partition.[41] Entries in the diary of Patel's daughter, Maniben Patel, confirm the dates and times of the meetings between her father and Menon, of which the latter speaks in his book. More details of Patel's conversion, and the reasons for it, can be found in my biography of the Sardar, published in 1991.[42]

From these and other accounts, we know that when in early June 1947 Mountbatten presented his Partition plan to India's political parties, leaders, and people, he did so with the knowledge that Patel and Nehru and the rest of the INC leadership would support the plan, and that Gandhi would not defy it.

Nehru saw Partition as painful but thought that rejecting the opportunity to govern a free, if smaller, India would be worse. This also seemed to be the general view across the country. Running all of undivided India in partnership with Jinnah and the Muslim League seemed an impracticable, unattractive, and almost impossible proposition.

This reading was confirmed by the unresolved strains in the interim Congress–League council, chaired by the Viceroy, which was in office between October 1946 and August 1947. Letting go of Muslim-majority parts and running the bulk of the land seemed preferable by far to Patel, Nehru, and their colleagues.

There were a few days in April 1947 when it seemed that Gandhi's idea of a united India with Jinnah as prime minister, presented by him on April 1 to the new viceroy, Lord Mountbatten, might take off. However, Nehru, Patel, and the rest of the INC leadership unequivocally opposed the idea. Unable to win the INC's leaders to his 'solution', a disappointed Gandhi withdrew himself from the negotiations for the transfer of power. In a letter he sent to Mountbatten on 11 April, Gandhi wrote:

> I had several short talks with Pandit Nehru, and an hour's talk with him alone, and then with several members of the Working Committee last night about the formula I had sketched before you, and which I had filled in for them with all the implications. I am sorry to say that I failed to carry any of them with me except Badshah Khan....
>
> I felt sorry that I could not convince them of the correctness of my plan from every point of view. Nor could they dislodge me from my position although I had not closed my mind against every argument. Thus, I have to ask you to omit me from your consideration. Congressmen who are in the Interim Government are stalwarts, seasoned

> servants of the nation, and, therefore, so far as the Congress point of view is concerned, they will be complete advisers.[43]

The 'Congressmen who are in the Interim Government' was a reference to Nehru, Patel, Azad, Prasad, Rajagopalachari, and Jagjivan Ram. The new Congress president, Kripalani, also favoured Partition.

Later that day (11 April), when two leaders of South Africa's Indians, Yusuf Dadoo and G. M. Naicker, called on him, Gandhi told them that while India no doubt stood 'on the threshold of independence', it was 'not the independence I want'. Added Gandhi:

> To my mind, it will be no independence if India is partitioned and the minorities do not enjoy security, protection, and equal treatment.... If what is happening today is an earnest of things to come after independence, it bodes no good for the future. I therefore feel ill at ease. But I

> am content to leave the future in God's good hands.[44]

Two days later, the Congress leaders formally 'scotched' Gandhi's idea. A diary entry on 13 April by C. R. reads: 'Gandhiji's ill-conceived plan of solving the present difficulties' was 'objected to by everybody and scotched'.[45] It was never put to Jinnah.

When word spread that Gandhi was not going to defy Nehru and Patel and would accept Partition, some reminded him of his 1940 statement—'Cut me to pieces first and then divide India'—and asked why he was not fasting against Pakistan.

These critics did not expect a Gandhi fast to change Jinnah's mind, or the minds of millions of Muslims in Muslim-majority areas who were looking forward to Pakistan, or the minds of non-Muslim leaders in Bengal and Punjab who wanted their provinces partitioned. But the prospect of Gandhi fasting and dying appealed to some Hindus who had never liked Gandhi's calls for Hindu-Muslim friendship, and who also disliked the Pakistan that was about to emerge. At his prayer meeting of 9 June, Gandhi addressed their sentiments:

> Lately I have been receiving a large number of letters attacking me. A friend points out how ineffective were my words when I said that vivisection of the country would be the vivisection of my own body.... When I said that the country should not be divided, I was confident that I had the support of the masses. But when the popular view is contrary to mine, should I force my own view on the people? ... I must step aside and stay back.[46]

In saying, 'the popular view is contrary to mine,' Gandhi was in effect also saying, 'when Patel, Nehru, and all the Congress leaders hold a contrary view'. Asking, 'Can I, should I, fast against Nehru, Patel, and all my associates of the last thirty years?' he answered himself by saying he couldn't. He wouldn't deny beloved comrades who had toiled, suffered, and sacrificed at his side the chance to lead India.

Moreover, the 'popular view' seemed to be for accepting Partition. This was confirmed at the mid-June meeting of the All-India Congress Committee that Nehru and party president Kripalani had pressed Gandhi to join. At this meeting, Gandhi openly asked the small number of Partition's vocal foes if they had the strength to defy the leaders:

> No one could be as much hurt by the division of the country as I am. And I don't think that anyone can be as unhappy today as I am….
>
> [I]f you feel that the Working Committee is in the wrong you should remove it, you should revolt and assume all power. You have a perfect right to do so, if you feel that you have the strength. But I do not find that strength in us today. If you

> had it, I would also be with you and if I felt strong enough myself I would, alone, take up the flag of revolt. But today I do not see the conditions for doing so....[47]

Would Gandhi have revised his stance of non-defiance if at this point delegates had cried, 'We are ready to revolt,' or 'Give us a lead, and we will fight'? There was no such demand. Not hearing a cry from the people of India against the proposed division, nor seeing an alternate set of Congress leaders willing and able to replace Nehru, Patel, and company, Gandhi chose to 'step aside and stay back'.

We may or may not like this piece of history, but history it was. In 1947, 'the entire nation' was not following Gandhi.

Neither the Hindu Mahasabha nor the RSS was politically strong in 1947. But there is little evidence that either of these organizations mounted an effort to stop the division or to strengthen Gandhi's hands for stopping it. The fact that Muslims remained in truncated India in 1947 annoyed the RSS and the Hindu Mahasabha much more than the emergence of Pakistan.

3

WHENCE THE REVENGE DRIVE?

'We were humiliated for 1,200 years. The Muslims and the British did horrible things. Finally, we have the chance to restore our ancient greatness.'

'Can anyone forget the Partition horrors?'

'Muslim appeasement proceeded unabated until 2014.'

'Hindus are finally running the land. History's wrongs are being righted. At last!'

We've been familiar with this music—I should call it 'this indignant music'—for years now. Local and national platforms play it. Unwelcome events like Donald Trump's tariffs and H-1B visa fees may intervene and for a while change the subject, but the song returns.

'The day of the Hindus has dawned. Minorities, especially Muslims and Christians, and maybe Sikhs too, should be put in their place.'

There are obvious problems with the message. The chief one is that yesterday, whether grand, horrible, mixed, or boring, was nonetheless yesterday. It has gone. Today is another day.

Moreover, learning from the past and avenging it are two different responses. The first is wise, the second hazardous and also unfair. Must today's Muslims, spread all over the land, pay in the year 2026 for what Mahmud of Ghazni did to the Somnath temple 1001 years ago, in 1025 CE? Should India's Christians suffer today for what the overzealous Portuguese did in Goa 400 years ago, in the sixteenth century?

'Of course not,' would be almost everyone's answer. If people are to be penalized for wrongs committed by forebears, no one would be left untargeted or unpunished. Since everyone's forebears were mistreated at some point or another in the past, should all of us spend our time looking for the offenders' descendants and squeezing apologies and restitution out of them? Will anyone have time left for any other task?

'Leave the past behind' has always been a foundational formula for sane living. Everywhere in the world.

Still, we should be aware of the strength with which the opposite opinion is held by elements influential in today's India. Muslims speaking of deprivations or attacks suffered by them are routinely advised to 'go to Pakistan'. Hindus are told that, in fact, they are the victims in Hindu-majority India. Alarm is regularly expressed at Muslim numbers in the land, and India's failure to compel its Muslims to become Hindus is openly lamented.

A 1994 book entitled *Threat of Islam: Indian Dimensions,* published in Mumbai by Unnati Prakashan and written by B. N. Jog, claimed that in an earlier century, Spain gave 'converted

Muslims the option either to return to their original fold of Christianity, or face death or expulsion from Spain'. The author complained that 'in India nobody even thought on the lines of Spain.... Hindus never thought of bringing back converted Muslims to their original Hindu fold. This serious lacuna resulted in keeping alive Islam.'[48]

Such reasoning may be ascribed to a fringe element and may not merit a response. However, Hindu nationalism's 'mainstream', which dwells on past humiliations and horrors—whether real, imagined, or exaggerated—should be required to answer a couple of questions.

Question number one: Did 'the Muslims' who invaded India from the northwest—first in the eleventh century, when Mahmud of Ghazni launched his raids; then in the thirteenth century, when Ghauri (or Ghori) established a kingdom in north India; and then again in the sixteenth century, when Babur's invasion started the Mughal empire—actually capture India? Or did India capture them?

Who really won and who really lost?

In recent years, histories taught to our children have been rewritten to claim that certain battles, thus far regarded as having been 'lost', were in fact, won. 'Celebrations' based on such 'corrections' are injurious to scholarship. They sow confusion in young minds, whose mandate in mathematics, biology, physics, and chemistry is to find the facts. Are they not expected to look for facts in history? Rewritings not based on facts will ensure that lessons on how battles are won or lost will not be learnt.

But my problem with the new history being taught is not confined to the rewriting projects. Why is it not underlined, I ask, that while a past battle may have placed a Delhi or Agra throne in Muslim hands, the expansion of Hindu ideas, Hindu practices, Hindu wealth, and Hindu numbers never ceased? In his 1967 book, *Indian*

Muslims, Muhammad Mujeeb quoted this lament of Sultan Jalaluddin Khilji, who reigned in Delhi from 1290 CE to 1296 CE:

> During our rule, the enemies of God and the enemies of the Prophet live under our eyes and in our capital in the most sophisticated and grand manner, in dignity and plenty, enjoying pleasures and abundance, and are held in esteem and honour among the Muslims.[49]

While Hindu chiefs indeed lost crucial battles and prestigious thrones, didn't India's Hindus emerge triumphant in the arguably more important wars of ideas, trade, and influence? Absorbing, assimilating, and occasionally transforming Muslim rule and Muslim rulers, the people of India frequently humbled the latter. Moreover, even as fortunate Hindus managed, under Muslim rule, to accumulate riches and bequeath them at will, Muslim nobles lost their wealth almost every time they displeased the Muslim king.

Who was winning? Who was losing? Who must now 'avenge'? Jalaluddin may have become numero uno, but who was gaining in the more important battle? Who eventually controlled the Indian mind and Indian resources?

Question number two: Dear Hindutva champions, when you say that ours was a wonderful past, I heartily agree, but I also ask for clarity. Please be good enough to describe, concisely if you can, the nature of our great past, and please be precise as well. Please *date* our past's finest periods.

When you talk about the great eras, what exactly are you referring to? Are you talking about the reign of Ashoka, approximately three centuries before the Common Era? Or are you referring to the rule of his grandfather, Chandragupta Maurya, which occurred some years prior, when the fabled Chanakya served as his mentor? The entire Maurya period, inclusive of Ashoka's reign, indeed saw a strong and unified state in India, but that state lasted less than 140 years. It was obliterated by Hindus, not by Christians or Muslims.

If you are speaking of a much earlier empire, say the one in India in 3400 BCE, of the kind recently popularized among Indians around the globe by the brilliant Amish Tripathi, please say that. In one of his latest novels, Amish offers parts of *his* story of *Raavan*, described as the *Enemy of Aryavarta*, who tries to vanquish Ram Chandra, the son of Emperor Dashrath, and Ram Chandra's peerless wife Sita.

Amish's story of Ram, Sita, and Raavan, to which he gives the date 3400 BCE, resembles but also contradicts other Ramayana versions. Most of these earlier renderings do not portray Dashrath as India's emperor, nor, to my knowledge, do any of them present Sita as an incarnation of Vishnu. In his novel, Amish does both.

He doesn't quite call Dashrath's kingdom 'India'. Borrowing a phrase from the Rig Veda, Amish calls the territory of action 'Sapta Sindhu', or the land of seven rivers. One of the Sapta Sindhu places readers of *Raavan* are introduced to is Salsette, the island on which the city of

Mumbai would later develop in the modern era. Predictably, Amish's readers also enter Lanka.

In some ways, the 3400 BCE empire painted for us by Amish is worth recreating. Among other things, this early empire possessed modern and 'reasonably soundproof' airliners, complete with seat-belts, 'portholes sealed with thick glass', and 'metallic window shades'.[50]

The fact that Amish is a writer of fiction does not mean that actual India was not marvellous in 3400 BCE. It merely confirms that the wonders and marvels of an ancient Indian empire have to be constructed wholly from imagination, not from historical evidence.

You may ask, are the Vedas not a marvel? They certainly are. Didn't the Vedas precede the Mauryan age by some or many centuries? According to the finest scholars, they probably did.

India's past *is* worthy of adoration and astonishment. Not because it contained a modern air force—it likely didn't—but because it saw staggering attempts to understand life on earth as well as the stars in the sky. We have firm evidence that in the span of time from say around 700 BCE to around 700 CE, a period of more than fourteen centuries, our thinkers, our astronomers, our mathematicians, our doctors, our debaters, our poets, and our grammarians displayed *extraordinary* gifts.

It was during that long period that the Ramayana and the Mahabharata were first written, Ashoka ruled, built his pillars, and had his rocks carved, and Panini composed his Sanskrit grammar and Patanjali his sutras. Later in that period, Aryabhatta explored the skies, and Harsha governed from Kannauj, where the Chinese scholar-pilgrim Xuanzang (Hiuen Tsang) called on him.

Our known history is a good deal older than that. Merely because more details have not yet been established about the amazing Harappan and Indus sites, dated to around 2400 BCE and found across a wide area, does not mean that ours was not a glorious past.

It *was* glorious—with one crucial flaw. Again and again in the flow of time, the India that we know from around 2400 BCE lacked *a large state*, one possessing rulers, institutions, laws, and officers enforcing the laws. Even in the two common era millennia that followed, such a state only existed sporadically.

The Harappan Civilization came, went, and was forgotten. Ashoka built his pillars, went, and was forgotten until the nineteenth century of the common era, when his edicts were deciphered. The Ajanta and Ellora caves were created, forgotten, 'lost' for centuries, and finally rediscovered.

No doubt the scroll of India's long history reveals a series of great kingdoms: the Mauryan empire; the Gupta kings of the north who enabled remarkable advances from the fourth to the sixth century CE; the Badami, Chaulukya, Chera, Chola, Hoysala, Kadamba, Pandyan, Pallava, Rashtrakuta, Satavahana and other dynasties competing in and from the peninsular south during the two common era millennia; the Palas of the east; the Vijayanagara empire that saw its peak in the sixteenth century in today's northern Karnataka; plus other impressive kingdoms and empires across the subcontinent, including the Sultanates of Delhi (thirteenth to sixteenth century CE) and the Mughal empire (sixteenth to nineteenth century).

However, these well-lit periods alternate in our history with *centuries* during which light is not cast by any lanterns of evidence, be they inscriptions, coins, other artefacts, or contemporaneous literature. In fact, obscure and stateless periods may have lasted longer on our soil than eras where a substantial state functioned.

The greatness of India's past is occasionally recalled by reminders of the phrase, 'sone ki chidiya', or the golden sparrow, which India certainly was from time to time. Robert Clive's companion, Robert Orme, who became a famed historian of the British empire, wrote in the 1760s that traders came to India for wealth, and mariners came to India for jobs, because of 'the magnificence of the richest empire of the globe'.[51]

In this perspective, the Mughals, whose empire was being described by Orme, emerge as builders of India's wealth and a source of pride, and not as a medieval horror requiring the humiliation of Muslims in twenty-first-century India.

Avengers should answer a precise question. We know that in the eighteenth and nineteenth centuries, the British replaced the Mughals as India's rulers. We know, too, that in the sixteenth century, the Mughals had defeated and replaced the Lodhis, the last dynasty of the Delhi Sultanate.

Do we know which Indian kingdom was replaced late in the twelfth century when Turkic Muslims under Muhammad Ghori defeated Prithviraj Chauhan in that critical 'Second Battle of Tarain' and thereafter commenced the Sultanate, starting what is often called the period of 'Muslim rule'?

Born in 1888 in the district of Gopalganj in what today is Bangladesh, Ramesh Chandra Majumdar became a distinguished historian. Champions of Hindu nationalism frequently cite him. In his reputed study, *Ancient India,* after telling the story of Prithviraj's victory over Ghori in Tarain's Battle One (1191 CE), and then of the Rajput hero's loss to Ghori in the following year in Battle Two—a loss facilitated by poor tactics and indiscipline on the Indian side—Majumdar offers these words:

'Thus ended the terrible day and the sun of Hindu glory set for ever on the fatal plain of Tarain (1192 AD).'[52]

Later called Taraori, the field of 'Tarain' is close to Haryana's well-known city of Karnal, which lies 110 km north of Delhi. Not long ago, these same battles of Tarain used to be described as Battles One and Two of Panipat (which is 25 kilometres south of Karnal) and connected to a Battle Three of Panipat, which was fought more than five centuries later on virtually the same ground.

In that 1761 battle, an invading force led by the Afghan, Ahmad Shah Abdali, also known as Ahmad Shah Durrani, defeated an overconfident Maratha army which showed up in North India and to which a dying Mughal empire had lent its feeble support.

Let's return to the Prithviraj saga, which has been kept alive through folk songs, plays, and films. Its romance is irresistible. The critical question is, however, almost never asked.

Of which portion of India was Prithviraj the king or emperor when he fought with Ghori, and for how long? In shorter words, which kingdom or empire did Ghori, or Ghori's Sultanate, replace? Which empire reflected the sun of glory that went down?

That is the core question. Once that is answered, we could ask about the empire's outstanding features and chief attainments. In available accounts, stories, and songs, Prithviraj is associated with Ajmer or Delhi or both, not with a glorious empire. In fact, we know very little of the extent, in time or in space, of Prithviraj's rule, or of the character of his chiefdom.

We know of contemporaneous rulers in other pockets in India where too, it seems, Ghori showed up with his soldiers—in Gujarat, in Kannauj (not far from modern Kanpur), in Kashi, and elsewhere. Some chiefs resisted Ghori, as Prithviraj had done. Some didn't. In short sentences, Majumdar tells the story—a mixed tale of daring, confusion, and ineptness.

Not a story of a unified kingdom resisting the invader. The inescapable conclusion is that there was no Indian empire for Ghori to replace.

Which is more important for us today? Avenging cruelties perpetrated by Ghori's soldiers in Ajmer in the year 1192—of which Majumdar gives a two-sentence picture—on today's Muslims in Ajmer or elsewhere? Or understanding why there was no unified Indian state at the end of the twelfth century? Or at other crucial periods in our history?

Written as a Sanskrit poem in the two years between 1148 and 1150 CE, i.e., well after Mahmud's depredations in Somnath but before Ghori's successes in different parts of India, Kalhana's *Rajatarangini* chronicles Kashmir's Buddhist and Hindu dynasties. Being a historical work, it is an exceptional treasure from our past, for while astronomy, mathematics, and medicine attracted our ancestors' minds, recording history did not. (China, by contrast, kept a detailed, generation-to-generation record of most of its regions.)

Curiously enough, while Kalhana in his twelfth century poem speaks of Mahmud of Ghazni and his battles with Hindu princes in the subcontinent's northwest, he is silent about the Somnath Temple or Mahmud's attack on it. Which underlines the absence in much of Indian history of anything like an India-wide grid or network—an Indian state or state-system—for registering and resisting incursions or invasions.

We miss an Indian state in earlier centuries too—in the long period that intervened between the Gupta dynasties and the invasions of Mahmud of Ghazni, and in the similarly long earlier span between the Mauryan empire and the Gupta kingdoms.

An Indian state is the Great Absence. As the eminent Indologist, A. D. Pusalker (1905–73), wrote in his 1951 book:

> All that we can say definitely is that Northern India was divided into a large number of states and, so far as our knowledge goes, no paramount power arose within this long period which could effectively exercise its supremacy over all or even a large number of them. We can dimly discern the struggles for supremacy … but we do not note any substantial progress towards the political unification of India.[53]

And yet, even without an Indian state, sooner or later, the people of India nullified an invasion and its consequences. To quote K. M. Munshi, 'The History of India is not the story of how she underwent foreign invasions, but how she resisted them and eventually triumphed over them.'[54]

Kanhaiyalal Maneklal Munshi (1887–1971) is an intriguing figure in recent Indian history. Popular novelist (in Gujarati), fighter for independence, minister in Congress governments, member of the Constituent Assembly, founder of the Bharatiya Vidya Bhavan network, and an ardent Hindu who, in the early 1940s, associated briefly with the Hindu Mahasabha, Munshi initiated, after independence, a project to recover ancient Indian history. The words quoted above are from his foreword, written in 1951, to the project's first volume, *The Vedic Age.* In that foreword, Munshi also said:

'Under the influence of European ideas and British democratic traditions, the Collective Spirit, without losing its grip over the essentials of its culture, adjusted itself to modern conditions, creating new intellectual and artistic movements, … seeking a secular democratic state, Indian in conception and technique.

[During Mughal rule] the world witnessed one of the most magnificent empires of all time.

British domination was a period of complete subjection, but it saw the national resurgence which, under Mahatma Gandhi, secured freedom by nonviolent means.

[F]oreign conquests which changed the course of history and the texture of life and culture … were only three. First, the Aryan conquests in prehistoric times which wove the essential pattern of national life and culture. Second, the Turko-Afghan conquests introduced Islamic influence into India and added new colours to the pattern of life. These conquests, however, soon lost their character of foreign military occupation, for the conquerors threw in their lot with the country and produced some of its best rulers and its most powerful political organizations....

Third, the British occupation from 1818 to 1947, perhaps the only period of foreign rule in the sense that the country was governed essentially by foreigners from a foreign country and in foreign interests. It brought in its wake contact with Europe, a new awakening, and a new cultural synthesis.

But during all this period, the vitality of the race and culture, altered from time to time in direction and objective, expressed itself with unabated vigour in resistance movements, military, political, and cultural. The History of India is not the story of how she underwent foreign invasions, but how she resisted them and eventually triumphed over them.'[55]

Munshi's 1951 perspective on history's invasions provides a helpful contrast to today's rage over Muslim rulers in a distant past and to the triumph shouted today every time an old Muslim name for a street, town, or railway station is erased.

It doesn't require time or effort to recognize that native divisions and follies—not external wickedness, whether Muslim or Christian—prevented stability in India. Native conflicts prevented the formation or continuance of kingdoms that provided order.

However, neither foreigners nor locals could prevent the flowering of Indian talent. We've had a proud history. Why then do we want revenge?

From the 1980s, when the campaign to remove the Babri Masjid was successfully launched, India's Hindus, i.e., the vast majority of the population, have been bombarded with the message that they and their ancestors have been the victims of an organized conspiracy to weaken them, and that the time has arrived for them to avenge themselves and reclaim their rightful place.

Not that Hindu victimhood was a new thought in the 1980s. It had been a major plank of the RSS ever since it started in the 1920s. But assertions of Hindu victimhood and the accompanying cry of appeasement of Muslims by India's governments reached high levels in the 1980s, and since then, the two claims have remained at that dominant altitude.

'Forcible conversion' has been a persistent staple of this propaganda. Earlier generations of India's Hindus did not swallow it. Despite their Muslimness, Akbar, the Taj Mahal, Dilip Kumar (whose real name was Yusuf Khan), and Nargis continued to receive Hindu love in the twentieth century, and Hindu parents continued to seek their children's admission into 'Christian' schools and colleges.

I am not speaking, though I could, of the pride that most Hindus entertain in the 2020s for contemporary stars in the sports or entertainment world whose Muslim, Sikh, or Christian affiliation is conveyed by their names. This pride goes against the theory that our fellow Muslims today are the result of forcible conversion yesterday.

Moreover, there's nothing to suggest that the anti-

Muslim anger reflected in some of today's headlines, whether directed at a mosque, dargah, or a name for a road or town, is the result of an experience or direct knowledge of forcible conversion or another misdeed perpetrated by Muslims.

The question that needs answering is this: why are so many Hindus with no personal experience of injury or unhappiness at Muslim hands comfortable with the notion of revenge against Muslims? Even, in the case of some, with a notion of forcibly converting Muslims into Hindus?

The revenge is being sought or exacted after a *huge* span of time. Mahmud's horrible raids occurred 1,000 years ago, Ghori attacked more than 800 years ago, and Babur 500 years ago. Not only that. Both Ghori and Babur bequeathed Indian kingdoms. Whether good, bad, or middling, the Sultanate and Mughal kings were Hindustani kings.

I am not a psychologist, but having observed fellow Indians and fellow Hindus in a longish lifetime, and having studied a little of our history, I may be allowed to offer my reading of this revenge wish.

'Before the Muslims and the British came, we had a glorious, in fact sublime, past.' This belief in a Mythic Past of Glory and Greatness is the foundation for our tolerance of injustices against our minorities today, injustices we explain away as the correction of historical wrongs.

'It is *their* karma. The Muslims and the Brits did horrible things. They must pay the price. Details of the terrible things don't matter. Can anyone forget the Partition horrors? In any case, we once had an incomparable past. Can anyone deny that? Foreigners derailed us. We were humiliated for 1,200 years. Now, finally, we have the chance to restore the ancient greatness.'

It is with 'reasoning' of this sort that we console and justify ourselves, and defend discrimination against minorities. Happiness at the belief—at the assumption, the ahistorical but pleasing assumption—that we were the first and the greatest is so intoxicating that we feel no need to check on its veracity.

If belief in a Mythic Past is central to the revenge drive, another component is our fascination with being 'number one'. 'What's your/her/his rank?' is a perennial curiosity in Indian life. It enters our thoughts and conversations, our hopes and plans, our careers and marriages, our disputes and conflicts, our joys and hurts, our ecstasies, and, saddest of all, the suicides of our youngsters.

Curiosity about rank is an element of human life everywhere, but in India, we give excessive and destructive prestige to the common urge to be ahead of others. In collective form, this unchecked urge has produced among us the hypothesis, not conducive to humility, that Indians were and are a chosen people, and that the world should recognize this 'fact'.

The respectability we've been giving in recent years to the laughable Vishwaguru notion is only one proof of our obsession with rank. The 'mother of democracy' claim is even more absurd. The fact that aspects of political democracy were on occasion debated in India even before the common era's start may be cause for a moment or two of legitimate pride, which, however, should quickly give place to shame.

Shame because of the social hierarchies (and social cruelties) India has tolerated for centuries, and also because of our failure to preserve an Indian state for more than a couple of centuries at a time.

Had love of rank been displaced by an interest in and respect for friends, associates, allies, and partners, India's kingdoms and governments—whether regional or national, ancient or modern—would have lasted longer in time.

Reluctance to laugh at ourselves may be part of the problem. Unwilling to smile at ourselves, we want to coerce others to cry or bow down before us. Taking ourselves too seriously may be why the Indian state, which depends on power-sharing among at least a few dominant groups, has broken up again and again in our history.

We defeat invaders when, yielding vanity, we laugh and unite with at least some of our Indian rivals. And when we learn the enemy's language.

We didn't do that when Ghori came, but many centuries later, we did. A while after British conquerors arrived, we learnt to unite, and we also learnt their language. The eventual results were indeed remarkable. Nehru and Gandhi, and many others who strove for liberty, were masters of English prose, even if most of them passionately championed Swadeshi.

This was a novel phenomenon in Indian history. The norm was, and continues to be, to make fun of other people's languages and accents, and of their physical appearance. It is another aspect of our sense of being the elect, the chosen. We did that with the Turkic and Arabic languages, and are now doing that with Mandarin or Chinese, although we dealt differently with the Brits.

As for our belief in an incomparable past, the remarkable Atharva Veda, the last of the Vedas, provides interesting light. It has a wonderful chapter on the Prithivi, i.e., on the earth, the land or geographical space where the community described in the Vedas, the Aryans, had been living, hunting and gathering for an unspecified and possibly long period.

The Atharva Veda's Prithivi or Earth chapter contains sixty-three stirring verses of gratitude for survival and flourishing. It also conveys a sense of wonder. Snow-clad mountains and rivers, cattle, horses, fields, grains, plants, herbs, potions, and minerals are mentioned. Available on the internet, a well-known Hindi translation (from the Sanskrit original) of this Prithivi chapter, published in Ajmer in 1980, gives the translated chapter the title *Matrubhoomi* (Motherland).

In his verse-by-verse rendering, the scholarly translator, Harivallabh Hari, frequently uses the word 'matrubhoomi', but I who can read Sanskrit without claiming to understand it can nowhere find the word 'matrubhoomi' in the Sanskrit verses he is translating. He appears to interpret Prithivi, Mother Earth, as Motherland.

This is not unreasonable. The verses breathe fervour and ardour towards the land described. The river Sindhu is specifically named. Various nature gods are mentioned too, including gods of fire and thunder.

But there is no ruler, no state, no police. No kingdom, no officers. There is the earth, there is nature, wonderful nature in fact, and a brave, energetic people—men, women, and children. But there is no state. There are a lower strata of people—the das or servants. Nonetheless there is ethics and morality, and there is virtue and honour and kindness. But there is no state. No Bharat, no Hindustan, no India. And there are no officers of the state. If there is a matrubhoomi here, it is Mother Prithivi or Prithvi, not, as yet, Bharat Mata or Mother India.[56]

~

In subsequent history, some invaders broke idols or seized them as treasure. This would surely have led to fierce resentment, but there is little evidence of the native population feeling that 'Islam' had won or that 'Hinduism' had lost. The native population always seemed aware of its huge advantage in numbers and of the invader's inescapable dependence, if he wished to stay, on native cooperation.

India's capacity to tame, absorb, and Indianize the invader was never in doubt. It was not pleasant to have the invader sitting on your native throne, but the new ruler was at times fairer in his rule than the one he replaced, provided stabler rule, and made India his home.

Did he capture India or had India accommodated and used him? Was the invader's success a national humiliation? Or did it offer scope for native resourcefulness, talent, and enterprise?

A reasonable retort to the narrative of an undated Mythic Past, followed by brutal invasion and humiliation, is that 'successful' invasions in fact were followed by assimilation and integration of Muslims in Hindu-majority India. Hindu India fully survived the Sultanate and the Mughals. Later it fully survived the Brits.

No doubt a Muslim ruler sat on the throne. And some Indians accepted Islam. However, the vast majority remained devoted to their traditional religious practices, a fact the ruler had to accept, whether he liked it or not. He could do nothing about it. He had been integrated.

Who had won and who had lost?

At times, Indian reaction to Muslim invaders or invasions—whether successful or repelled—was couched in anger. It included calling the invaders 'mlecchas' or barbarians. The reaction seldom seemed to refer to Islam or to a fight over religious beliefs or practices. The focus was on the invaders' 'impure' race and their destructiveness. Being outsiders was enough to earn the label of impurity. Frequently, however, their warring skills were acknowledged.

And when stable rule followed, there were remarkable consequences. It was in the sixteenth century, at the height of Mughal glory, with Emperor Akbar on the throne, that the saint-poet Tulsidas composed his Ramcharitmanas, one of Hinduism's most revered and most popular texts. Today, in the twenty-first century, more than 500 years after Akbar's death, millions of Hindu families continue to rear their children on the stories, morals, dilemmas, and lessons provided by Tulsidas's long poem.

In Ramcharitmanas, the poet calls Rama, among other titles, 'Gharib-Nawaz', the Persian-Arabic phrase denoting the Benefactor of the Poor.

Can anyone possibly argue that tyranny or horror is a truer, longer-lasting child of the Mughal era than Ramcharitmanas?

A century before Tulsidas and Akbar, at the end of the Sultanate, the poet Kabir had injected into the Indian mind an awareness that Hindu/Muslim, native/foreigner, and high-caste/low-caste were false distinctions. Kabir's presence in India's history does not signify subjugation. On the contrary, he symbolizes a synthesis of two cultures as also an advance in humanity's understanding of itself.

Centuries after Kabir, Gandhi's confidence in Hinduism was unaffected by 1,200 years of rule by non-Hindus. Nor did he compose diatribes against Islam or Christianity. He tried to create a nation out of unconnected and often alienated segments. He tried to reform Hindu society and bring justice to it. And he hoped that free India's leaders would refashion, in the interests of India's humble majority, the state which the British had built on the foundations of the Hindostan organized earlier by the Mughals.

Eight decades later, in the 2020s, our priority tasks are no different. Strengthening the Indian nation by deepening its internal bonds. Continuing the reformation of Indian society and the removal of its injustices. And demanding the humanization of the Indian state.

Compared with those tasks, putting the country's Muslim and Christian minorities in their place seems a harsh, petty, and undignified activity.

4

HINDUS ON PLANET EARTH

Our earth is peopled by humans on the move. And may always have been. Were there periods anywhere in the world when families, clans, or tribes remained fixed to one place for more than a couple of lifetimes? Our most compelling 'traditional' stories, wherever we live, seem to be about journeys and also, quite often, about exile. The thought of home brings tears, but the sweat of travel brings opportunities. An opportunity or a compulsion may create a home in a totally different place, near or far, which may evoke smiles or fresh tears. That's the story of human life on earth.

As a subject for study on college campuses in India, migration may not be as exciting as colonialism. As a historical process, migration has lasted longer. The British empire came to

India and then went away. Only a tiny number of Brits, a mere handful, made India their home. A much larger number of Indians, who would fill God knows how many steamers and aircraft, moved to Britain and made it their long-term home.

Their grandchildren and great-grandchildren too are likely to make the UK their home, unless they see better prospects in Europe or North America or elsewhere. With people from places other than India also relocating in the 'Western world' (an ecosystem geographically larger than Europe or North America), migration has become a hot subject for study on campuses there.

The expanding Indian footprint on far corners of our earth is preponderantly a Hindu stamp. This is important to recognize. In recent years, India's Muslims, around 15 per cent of the population, may have had a stronger reason to migrate out of India, but they face bigger hurdles along the way. An average Muslim in India is not only poorer than the average Hindu, he or she is less likely, given Islamophobia's global rise, to obtain entry in a prosperous country.

Places like the Gulf countries and Malaysia are exceptions to this generalization. Being a Muslim is not a handicap when Indians apply for a visa to a Gulf nation or to Malaysia. However, even among Indians moving to these countries, Hindus easily outnumber Muslims.

In short, in our earth as a whole, the migrating Indian is usually a Hindu. Hindus have circled the earth the way a temple or an idol is circumambulated by the devout. They are on a global yatra, a parikrama or pradakshina, a pilgrimage that may not, however, conclude with a return to the starting point.

In the nineteenth century, under colonial auspices, a large number of very poor Indians had moved, often as serfs or semi-serfs, to places like Mauritius, Fiji, South Africa, Guyana, Trinidad, and Jamaica. Willingness to work hard and take risks enhanced their living standards. Political struggles raised their civic status. More and more parts of the world saw Indians living in their midst.

In the twentieth century, many more Indians, i.e., many more Hindus, embraced the globe beyond India. Having Hindus as neighbours became a common experience for people in Africa, North and South America, Europe, Australia and New Zealand. Except for a small number of Indians in South Africa who became Christian, almost all other migrating Indians retained their Hindu faith, or their Muslim, Sikh, Christian, or Zoroastrian beliefs.

Countries like the US, proud of their independence, nationalistic in varying degrees but curious about other faiths and generally committed to freedom of belief, were inclined to see an immigrating Indian as a Hindu rather than an Indian. Or as a Muslim, Sikh, or Christian rather than an Indian.

The fact that for a long-time indigenous Americans or Canadians were spoken of as 'Indians' was one reason for characterizing people from India as Hindus. Whereas 'Hindu American' was a clear category, 'Indian American' could confuse. Rather than denoting people from India, the phrase could suggest the American 'Indians' whose ancestors had made the Western Hemisphere their home thousands of years ago.

Even today, people from India are, at times, called '*East* Indians' in the US, differentiated by that prefix from descendants of the 'original' Indians of the Western world who, if they had survived the impact of European conquest and migration, had been pushed into reservations.

There's some similarity in how Hindus, Muslims, and Jews have been viewed in the US. Thus, one often hears, in the state of New York and elsewhere on the US East Coast, of nineteenth-century Italian, Irish, and Jewish immigrants. The last named might have come from Russia, Poland, Ukraine, Belarus, Lithuania, Austria, Hungary, or some other country. Yet they are described as Jews, and not by their earlier nationality. They're seldom called Polish or Hungarian immigrants or given another 'national' prefix. Italian and Irish immigrants, on the other hand, are spoken of in that way and are not called 'Catholic' immigrants.

Although the phrase 'Indian immigrant' is more common in the US than 'Hindu immigrant'—just as the expression 'Afghan immigrant' or 'Syrian immigrant' is more widely used than 'Muslim immigrant'—Hindu identity rivals Indian identity in the minds of immigrants and onlookers alike. An Afghan or Syrian identity similarly melds, in the US, into a Muslim identity.

While usually a Hindu, an Indian outside India can, of course, be a Sikh, Christian, Muslim, or Zoroastrian instead, or an adherent of another religion. The opposite probability, of a non-Indian being a Hindu, is low. True, she could be a Nepali, a Bangladeshi, a Sri Lankan Tamil, or a Hindu Sindhi from Pakistan. Or a descendant of Indians by way of Trinidad, Guyana, or Suriname. Or, of course, a descendant of forebears who had migrated more recently from India to the US,

Britain, Canada, France, Germany, Australia, whatever.

Black Hindus, however, or white Hindus, or Hindus of say Chinese, Japanese, Arab, or Turkic descent, do not seem to exist in significant numbers. Not as of now, at any rate. A high-profile exception to this 'rule' is Trump's director of national intelligence, Tulsi Gabbard. While Tulsi's mother is a white American of European extraction, her father has European as well as Samoan roots. Converting to Hinduism before Tulsi was born, her mother, Carol Porter Gabbard, raised her daughter as a Hindu.[57]

A 2023–24 study of 'the religious landscape' of the US, done by the Pew Research Center, found that 0.9 per cent of American adults saw themselves as Hindus.[58] That would mean that about 2.8 million Hindu adults currently live in the US. While the vast majority are of Indian descent, another Pew survey indicated that 9 per cent of US Hindus belong to a non-Asian ethnicity, divided into whites (4 per cent), blacks (2 per cent), Latinos (1 per cent), and mixed (2 per cent).[59]

Pew also found that in the course of a decade, from 2010 to 2020, the number of Hindus living in the world's 'Middle East-North Africa' region, to which the Gulf nations belong, rose by 62 per cent to touch 3.2 million. In North America, the Hindu population grew by 55 per cent to 3.6 million.[60] Europe also saw a considerable increase, to 2.2 million (a 30 per cent rise).

These were dramatic additions. Numbers thereafter would have risen further, and perhaps as steeply. Such figures bring up the intriguing question: is 'Hindu' then an ethnic or genetic label, related more to your birth, to where you and your forebears were born, than to your beliefs?

Researching twenty-five years ago for a paper on 'Hinduism and Peacebuilding', I found the following sentence in a 1966 book by D. S. Sarma, a South Indian scholar closely connected to the Ramakrishna Mission: 'At times seeming a religion more of birth or race than of belief, [Hinduism] has been called an "ethnic religion … which grew along with the nation that gave birth to it.'"[61]

What is an ethnic religion? We can look at Zoroastrianism, the religion associated with the Parsis of India and of Iran. It was founded around the seventh century BCE by Zarathushtra, more often called Zoroaster. The gifted Parsis of India and Iran belong to small Zoroastrian communities, many of whose members have moved in recent decades to North America, the UK, and Australia.

Having travelled to many continents in a long lifetime, I've run into people of a hundred varieties, but not so far into a Zoroastrian who was not a Parsi. Marriage outside the Parsi community seems frowned upon, and conversion of non-Parsis to Zoroastrianism is never attempted. Zoroastrianism appears to have remained an ethnic religion.

In contrast, a Christian could be from Alaska, Zimbabwe, or any other place on the globe. He or she could possess a skin-colour or facial appearance of any sort. Almost the same is true for Muslims, who, however, are concentrated in the Middle East, North Africa, and South and Southeast Asia. Clearly, Christianity and Islam are not ethnic religions.

The world's Buddhists, around 500 million in all, are outnumbered by the world's Hindus, who today total around 1.2 billion. Still, there are at least thirteen countries, large and small, where Buddhists comprise either a majority or at least a tenth of the population: China, Japan, North Korea, South Korea, Mongolia, Thailand, Vietnam, Cambodia, Laos, Myanmar, Sri Lanka, Bhutan, and Nepal.

Hindus form a majority or more than 10 per cent of the population in the following twelve countries: India, Nepal, Bhutan, Sri Lanka, Mauritius, Fiji, Suriname, Guyana, Trinidad, Kuwait, Qatar, and the UAE.

The Hindu percentage in the populations of the US, the UK, France, Germany, Canada, or Australia is well under 10. Each of these countries, however, contains an impressive and growing number of Hindus. Given the global influence of the six countries named, their Hindus can be credited with considerable potential. Which is not to say that Hindus in the rest of the world are less important.

The impact on humankind of its 1.2 billion Hindus is a question worth thinking about. What do these 1.2 billion men, women, and children believe? Or believe in? Are they Hindus because of their beliefs or because of where they were born? What principles or values do they cherish? In what way or ways does their religion guide their lives day by day? How does it aid them in times of difficulty? Does their faith instruct them on their relations with the rest of humankind?

Such is the discussion these pages have hoped to provoke.

We should mark that Hindus living in India, who still constitute, despite all the moving about we have observed, the great bulk of the earth's Hindus, are acutely interested in the wider world. Even a minor incident involving an Indian in a country like the US can go viral across India, can make headlines in large or small newspapers all over India. In fair part, this is connected to the wish in many young Indians for a chance in life elsewhere. What Indians do elsewhere on earth, and what is done to Indians elsewhere, matters to people within India.

Moreover, a fair percentage of India's inhabitants now have close relatives living outside India whom they see and talk to regularly over the phone. Our feet may be on India's good earth but our eyes and ears are everywhere on planet Earth.

While some migrating Indians have married outside their race, a majority still appear to marry an Indian, often an Indian of their caste, who could be from their new home or from the motherland. Non-Indian spouses of Hindu

Indians cannot be sure of easy acceptance in the Hindu community. When visiting India, they often have difficulty entering a temple's sanctum sanctorum. To many temple priests, a white Hindu, or the even less common black Hindu, or a Japanese or Chinese Hindu, is an anomaly if not an impostor.

As D. S. Sarma noted six decades back, Hinduism conveys traits of an ethnic religion. While a Hindu not of the Indian race thus remains an unusual sight, the Tulsi Gabbards of our world are real.

There is pushback to the Indians' and Hindus' global spread. The $100,000 fee for work visas that US President Donald Trump announced on 19 September 2025, was not India-specific, but Indians have constituted 70 per cent of all H-1B visa recipients in recent years. The $100,000 fee may have a complicated and unpredictable future, but it can be seen as being, among other things, a numerical expression of the opposition to immigration, including immigration from India.[62]

There has been speculation that the gigantic fee is temporary and only a bargaining ploy to extract the free entry of dairy and wheat into India or some other concession.

Apparently, Trump claimed that the global tech industry, the biggest consumer of H-1B visas, would not oppose the move. His Commerce Secretary, Howard Lutnick, said that 'all big companies' were on board with the fee hike. Lutnick added that the change would likely result in far fewer H-1B visas than the 85,000 annual cap because 'it's just not economic anymore.'

'If you're going to train people, you're going to train Americans,' Lutnick told reporters. 'If you have a very sophisticated engineer and you want to bring them in … then you can pay $100,000 a year for your H-1B visa.'[63]

The White House issued a major clarification: the $100,000 fee will be a 'one-time' payment imposed on new applicants. 'This is a one-time fee that … only applies to new visas, not renewals or current visa holders,' a White House official said.

But discomfort with Indian inflow is unmistakable. Two weeks prior to the $100,000 fee announcement, one of America's most popular TV hosts, Laura Ingraham of Fox News, had tweeted: 'Don't forget that any trade deal with India will require us to give them more visas. I'd rather not pay them in visas…. Let Modi see what terms he can get from Xi instead.'

Ingraham's not-so-friendly comments were immediately amplified by Charlie Kirk, the Trump supporter and founder of Turning Point USA, who would be killed a few days thereafter (on 10 September 2025) while addressing a students' rally in Utah. Accusing Indian professionals of displacing American workers, Kirk underscored Ingraham's warning and tweeted as follows:

'America does not need more visas for people from India. *Perhaps no form of legal immigration has so displaced American workers as those from*

India. (Italics added.) Enough already. We're full. Let's finally put our own people first.'

Evidently, the combined tweets of Kirk and Ingraham drew 9.9 million views.[64]

Can anyone now remember the time when it was imagined that Indians in the US were being accepted as some kind of 'model minority'?

The most gruesome story was the murder on 10 September 2025, in a Dallas motel of the Indian manager, forty-one-year-old Chandra Nagamallaiah, by a man named Yordanis Cobos-Martinez, who was described as an illegal immigrant from Cuba with a history of previous crimes. In front of his wife and child, Nagamallaiah's head was severed by a machete and kicked around. Among the many who condemned the grotesque crime was Ro Khanna, the US Congressman of Indian origin from California, who posted this on X:

'The brutal beheading of a hardworking Indian American immigrant in front of his wife & son is horrific. The murderer had multiple prior arrests for violent theft & child endangerment & was undocumented. He should not have been free on American streets.'[65]

The story sickened everyone it reached, and hearts went out to the child and the widow, but it also confirmed the sobering fact that sections of the American public harbour dislike and resentment for Indian immigrants.

Posting a video of Indians boisterously celebrating a festival in his residential 'colony'—to use the Indian expression for what suburban Americans call a 'sub-division'—a white American added these words: 'Typical view in my neighborhood outside Dallas. We have to cancel the H1-Bs. I want my kids to grow up in America. Not India.'[66]

The blueprint of a race-blind Beloved Community that Martin Luther King had presented to America may now survive only in some inaccessible basement.

Blocking migration is not merely an American wish. It has become a worldwide urge. Capitalizing on Kirk's assassination, Tommy Robinson, founder of the 'English Defense League', organized, on 14 September 2025, a London rally of 110,000 (perhaps more) white Britons where an end to immigration was demanded. Elon Musk spoke to this rally, which was also addressed by European foes of immigration.

The far-right French politician, Eric Zemmour, told those who had gathered in London, 'We [the French and the British] are both subject to the same process of the great replacement of our European people by peoples coming from the south and of Muslim culture. You and we are being colonized by our former colonies.'[67]

Robinson and Zemmour both underlined the Muslim element in the migration to Europe and the UK, to which the emotional phrase, 'The Great Replacement', has now been attached. Interestingly, in a post-rally interview to an Indian TV channel, Robinson, whose original name was Stephen Yaxley-Lennon, expressed admiration for Modi, contempt for Pakistan ('Nothing good has come from there'), and said he wanted Balochistan 'freed'.[68]

Delighted by his remarks, many Indian viewers praised Robinson in online comments. India's Hindus may blunder, however, if they imagine that resentment against immigrants in the US, Canada, the UK, and Australia is limited to Muslims. For the bulk of the population in these countries, 'people from India' are just that, and part of the 'replacement' spectre. Their being Hindu, Sikh, Muslim or anything else makes little difference.

Australia. Between 2013 and 2023, the number of Indians permanently migrating to Australia more than doubled, reaching, at the end of June 2023, the figure of 845,800, which constituted 10.3 per cent of all overseas-born Australians and 3.2 per cent of Australia's total population. These numbers, which did not include students, visitors, and other Indians residing temporarily, would have grown in the period after June 2023. After India, the countries of origin for permanent residents in Australia, ranked by numbers exported, were China, the Philippines, Nepal, the UK, Pakistan, Vietnam, Sri Lanka, and South Africa.[69]

On 31 August and 1 September 2025, protests organized under a 'March for Australia' banner took place in major Australian cities, including Sydney, Melbourne, Adelaide, and Brisbane. Tens of thousands of people attended these rallies.

While the overall focus of these rallies was on ending mass migration, Indian immigrants were specifically named in protest material. Flyers claimed that in five years, more Indians had arrived in Australia than Greeks and Italians in a hundred years.

The Australian government and prominent political figures condemned the rallies, calling them hateful, racist, and divisive. Investigators linked the rallies to right-wing extremism and neo-Nazi groups. Members of the Indian-Australian community said they felt targeted and disappointed by the hostile rhetoric, which ignored the significant contributions migrants make to Australia's economy and society.

Far-right or racist thinking about Indians in Australia seems to have drawn support from uncorroborated social media stories demeaning Indians. One such story alleged collusion among Indian nurses, taxi drivers, and real estate agents to provide the agents with addresses of older patients.

The Australian Broadcasting Corporation reported that the 'March for Australia' website had at first demanded a 'remigration' policy. Thickly associated with the White Australia movement, that phrase was later deleted. Added the ABC: 'Remigration is a notion linked to far-right ideology that calls for the mass deportation of non-European peoples from Western nations.... "March for Australia" maintains that its opposition to current immigration levels is not "far-right".'

Directly or indirectly, 'March for Australia' charged that immigrants from India were adding to housing shortages, job insecurity, declining productivity, environmental decay, lowered living standards, and the erosion of national identity.

'So, protect Australian heritage, culture, way of life. Next step, protect European culture, heritage, way of life. The next step is to protect white heritage.' This seemed to be the call.[70]

Some weeks later, Anne Aly, Australia's minister for Cultural Affairs, offered a different perspective. Visiting Delhi, Aly told Divya A. of the *Indian Express* that her prime minister, Anthony Albanese, had assured Indian-Australians that the country welcomed them and acknowledged that they 'make our country stronger by being here'. Aly also said:

> I am Australia's first standalone Cabinet Minister for Multicultural Affairs. Over half of Australians were either born overseas themselves or have a parent

> who was born overseas. I'm one of them. I came to Australia from Egypt as a toddler and grew up in Sydney's western suburbs, surrounded by neighbours from all corners of the world. We played street cricket with garbage-bin wickets—and as day turned to night, every child's name called out to come to dinner came with a different accent. That was Australia to me.[71]

The last month of 2025 saw the horrific shooting in Sydney's famed Bondi Beach by a father-and-son duo of Indian origin. At least 15 Jewish Australians who had gone to the beach to celebrate a Jewish festival were gunned down. Some lives were probably saved by the fearless bravery of an Australian Muslim of Syrian origin who snatched the gun of one of the killers, but the Sydney shooting will not make it easier for many more Indians to settle in Australia.

In electoral constituencies in the Western world that contain sizable chunks of Hindu voters, using anti-Muslim rhetoric to win Hindu support is tempting for far-right 'locals'. Such rhetoric is unlikely, however, to translate into pro-Hindu policy. Not without a major convulsion.

As of now, no one in any country is offering to lower visa fees for Hindu Indians or remove other hurdles for them. Nor can anyone make that kind of discriminatory offer under current legal and constitutional systems in the US, the UK, Canada, Australia, New Zealand, or countries of the European Union.

People like Laura Loomer, a far-right political activist in the US, are exceptions. In an internet slanging match on 26 October 2025 with the UK-born Mehdi Hasan, who is a well-known media personality in the US, Loomer insisted that 'our problem isn't with brown people. It's with Islam.'

Annoyed with criticism Hasan had made of Vice President J. D. Vance, Loomer told him via

X: 'Vance's wife isn't a Muslim. If she was, he never would have been Vice President.' Unaware of Hasan's Indian origins (both his parents hail from Hyderabad), Loomer flung this at him: 'You are a Muslim immigrant. You can go back to the UK and the Islamic countries your parents were born in any time you want.' In response, Hasan duly corrected Loomer on his parents' first nationality.[72]

Wherever they live—in India, the US, the UK, Australia, Canada, or anywhere else—India's Hindus will need to figure out if they really want to climb onto the 'white first' and anti-Muslim platform of people like Robinson, Zemmour, and Loomer. That stage is where many far-right Americans—or Canadians, Australians, or others —may be found, too, but it is also where, in the end, there will be no respect for Indians of any kind.

The alternative is to throw our weight in favour of a world in which, regardless of race or creed, all will live as equals and friends.

India's long history of respect for different faiths and traditions, the unique texture of India's anti-colonial struggle, and India's constitution all point in one direction. Given, however, the persistence of anti-Muslim tirades in India, it is hard to predict the path that India's Hindus will take.

Ireland. Migrants from India have run into unexpected dislike in Ireland as well. In a brilliant article in *The Guardian* of Britain, the novelist Cauvery Madhavan, a first-generation citizen in Ireland, offered practical tips for coping:

> I say, stop with the handwringing. Extend those same hands instead in friendship—at a bus stop, on a train, at work. Try small talk with the person in a hospital, at the school gates. A smile in a supermarket queue is more reassuring than any grand political statement. We are good at talking about the weather. Do it, it breaks barriers. Commit to

> random acts of friendliness. Return to being neighbourly, be nosy even.[73]

To return to the question raised earlier, are our earth's Hindus more Hindu than Indian? Or Indian more than Hindu? For one influential Hindu, the question makes no sense. It is irrational. Mohan Bhagwat, the RSS chief, thinks that Hindu and Indian are synonymous terms. Responding in October 2025 to a question from Jim Geraghty, one of America's prominent conservative writers, who was meeting him in RSS's headquarters in Nagpur, Bhagwat said:

'There is no non-Hindu Indian, there is no non-American American. "Hindu" refers to all the people of India, not just those of the Hindu religious faith … Christian, Muslim, you are the sons of this land, the same descendants of our ancestors.'

Geraghty quoted this conversation in a *Washington Post* article published on 14 October 2025. He added: 'When asked whether Pakistan is Hindu under his definition, Bhagwat responds, 'Naturally—same ancestors.' Asked why there is such strife between India and Pakistan, Bhagwat answers, 'Ignorance of this.'

'My trip,' Geraghty duly disclosed, 'was sponsored by the Hudson Institute and the Foundation for India and Indian Diaspora Studies, whose president is affiliated with RSS.'[74]

For Bhagwat, therefore, Hinduism is ethnic. It's a label. A fact decided by your bloodline. It does not seem to depend on what you believe. Nor on how you think you should live your life. You are born into Hinduism and with Hinduism. Your mind might choose to believe in the Buddha or in Jesus, or believe that Muhammad represented the culmination of prophethood. However, since your ancestors were Indian, you are a Hindu.

You may be an extremist somewhere in Pakistan, ready to use terror as a weapon against India, but your ancient ancestors were Hindu and so you are a Hindu, whether or not you admit it.

What if you are a naturalized Indian citizen, an Indian per the Constitution, which states that if you have entered India lawfully and lived in India for a minimum number of years, you become an Indian? By now, there are a decent number of Indians of this kind. But since their forebears were not Indian, they are not and cannot be Hindu by Bhagwat's definition even if they want to be, or think they are.

These pages have not been concerned with the laws or rules of citizenship. They are about the practices and beliefs that make someone a Hindu. Among other things, they dispute Bhagwat's contention that Hinduism is primarily and only a matter of where you are born, of the blood or genes you inherited.

Even if we go along with Bhagwat and assume

that the vast majority of India's Muslims and Christians, and the vast majority of the people of Pakistan and Bangladesh, are Hindus, since centuries ago their forebears were Hindus, there are questions to ask.

Are we the Hindus of India as tolerant and understanding as we should be of our fellow Hindus who 'mistakenly' call themselves Muslims or Christians or Pakistanis or Bangladeshis? When needed we must be tough with the governments of Pakistan and Bangladesh; but should we wipe out from our minds the people of Pakistan and Bangladesh, who are not only our neighbours but also, as Bhagwat informs us, our fellow Hindus?

The final question is connected not to Shri Bhagwat but to the ancient, anonymous, and amazing composer of the 'Vasudhaiva Kutumbakam' phrase. If the Muslims, Christians, Sikhs, Buddhists, and Parsis of India are members of our family, i.e., our relatives, are these relatives receiving from us the treatment that relatives deserve?

Actually, Vasudhaiva Kutumbakam would require us to think of the people living in Dhaka, Lahore, Karachi, Peshawar, and similar places as our relatives too.

5

TWO ROADS BEFORE HINDUS

Let me sum up what I've wished to say.

Firstly, Hindus having spread all across the globe, Hinduism is no longer fused with the Indian landmass. It exists outside India as well, even though Hindus not of an Indian race are yet to constitute a vast number. For the foreseeable future, a large majority of the world's Indians will probably be Hindus, and a large majority of the world's Hindus will probably be Indian. That will still mean a great many Indians who are not Hindu and possibly a significant number of non-Indian Hindus.

My second point was more of a question than a statement. Will Hindu values come to the fore in the world's mind? With time, will Hindu values be distinguished more plainly from the

Hindu race, enabling all of humanity to access the values with a clear mind? We should, in particular, ask if non-Indian spouses or partners of Hindu Indians will find more precise notions of Hindu values.

Thirdly, we should recognize that Indians and Hindus are being observed and studied by others. Is the world watching the Hindu race's growth with curiosity? With gladness? With hope? Or with concern, fear, or even hostility? In part, the answer is connected to how we Hindus conduct ourselves in India and outside, and on how the Hindu majority and government agencies treat India's religious minorities.

On this last question, the state of affairs is widely known. It is not pretty. Incident upon incident induces sadness and more than sadness. Including shock, disgust, anger, and shame. At times, the treatment is inhuman. Usually, and most troublingly, there is only silence in response. No rebuke, dissociation, or corrective is voiced from a governmental platform. Or on behalf of the ruling party. Just as disappointingly, leaders of Hindu religious organizations choose to remain quiet.

For sincere Hindus, this double whammy of assault followed by silence is shattering. For non-Hindus curious about Hinduism, the incidents are disillusioning and off-putting.

We have become familiar with the pattern. Mobilized by WhatsApp, a mob attacks a Muslim for allegedly storing beef or for hurting Hindu sentiments in some other way. The police pursue not the attackers but the victim's relatives to check if the mob's accusations are valid. Courts are slow or reluctant to intervene. Exceptions apart, the media suppresses, downplays, or twists an attack. Political and religious leaders find ways to justify it.

Livelihoods may be snatched from humble Muslim tailors or vendors of street food. Or a mosque or a dargah may be rendered vulnerable by claims that it conceals a Hindu shrine. No punishment or even condemnation follows. Protests by victims or their sympathizers can invite *their* arrest.

Because they protested, a large number of Muslims are in fact behind bars across India. Many have remained there for years, without trial or bail.

Because such sequences have been continually repeated, India's Muslims are frightened and deeply insecure. The state of Christians is not much better either.

Many will remember the video that surfaced in August 2023 in which a woman teaching in a school in western UP's Muzaffarnagar district asked schoolboys to hit their seven-year-old Muslim classmate for 'not memorizing his lessons'. According to the boy's father, the teacher 'asked the [classmates] to slap my son one by one', which the children proceeded to do. The teacher also declared that Muslim children should not have been admitted into the school. The boy went home crying.

It seems that this teacher may have apologized later to the boy's parents, although in remarks to others she defended her behaviour.[75] Sections of the media reported the incident, but no public chastisement emerged from any UP minister or any member of the Union cabinet. No one representing the schools of UP or connected with organized teaching in India's most populous state spoke up.

In short, millions saw a seven-year-old boy being humiliated in his class by his teacher, who enlisted the boy's classmates in the humiliation. In response, the Indian establishment's leaders and elders remained silent!

Long ago, in his *Experiments with Truth,* Gandhi recalled an incident from the year 1894, when he was a twenty-four-year-old lawyer in Durban, South Africa. After being beaten roughly by his white master, a Tamil-speaking indentured labourer named Balasundaram had sought young Gandhi's help. The latter was able to obtain Balasundaram's transfer to another master. After relating the story, Gandhi wrote:

> It has always been a mystery to me how men can feel themselves honoured by the humiliation of their fellow beings.[76]

It is a fact that noticeable numbers of vocal Hindus in contemporary India feel themselves temporarily elated and energized by the humiliation of helpless Muslims. Hindus who feel let down and embarrassed are more numerous. However, most of us remain silent, for speaking out can invite trouble.

Hindus, therefore, have work to do. Not coming to the aid of the weak or the endangered is not a value that Hindus were taught to prize.

On the night of 28 November 2023, relief was felt across India when, one by one, forty-one men, who were trapped in a tunnel in Uttarakhand, came out alive after seventeen days of suspense.

What were the names of the twelve toilers who, after giant machines failed, had dug with their hands, fingers, and nails the hole through which the trapped men surfaced? Monu, Naseer, Ankur, Jatin, Saurabh, Feroz, Munna Quereshi, Rashid, Irshad, Naseem, Wakeel Hassan, and Devender.[77] Some of them Hindus, some of them Muslims, all humble diggers and labourers.

Bound together by the precariousness of their lives.

And by their Hindu value, the Muslim value, the human value of insaniyat.

Perhaps the question is of where our minds travel. We can climb vertically into our imagined past, and savour the presumed glory there. Or we can enter horizontally into the lives of our compatriots, our neighbours of different castes and creeds, and see if we can lower the pain we may find there.

To both exercises we seem to give the name Hinduism. May we choose the benevolent one.

ENDNOTES

1 'Nine Beliefs of Hinduism', *Hinduism Today*, 6 February 2020.

2 *Om Jai Jagdish Hare* Aarti with Hindi, English lyrics by Anuradha Paudwal. https://www.youtube.com/watch?v=NE3SWh9_vR4

3 'Geeta Saar (Essence of the Geeta)', available on https://theory.stanford.edu/~sbansal/geeta_saar/geeta_saar.html

4 'Swami Vivekananda and His 1893 Speech', Art Institute of Chicago.

5 Sugata Bose, *His Majesty's Opponent*, Cambridge, Massachusetts: Harvard University Press, 2011, p. 327.

6 Ibid., p. 299.

7 Manu Gandhi, *Ekla Chalo Re*, Ahmedabad: Navajivan, pp. 91–92.

8 Vinoba Bhave, *Moved by Love*, Hyderabad: Sat Sahitya Sahayogi Sangh,1994, p. 287.

9 *Harijan*, 20 October 1940; *Collected Works of Mahatma Gandhi*, vol. 73, pp. 104–05.

10 Gopalkrishna Gandhi (ed.), *Gandhi is Gone: Who Will Guide Us Now? Nehru, Prasad, Azad, Vinoba, Kripalani, JP, and Others Introspect, Sevagram, March 1948*, Ranikhet: Permanent Black, 2007, p. 66.

11 Ibid., pp. 76–77.

12 Ibid., pp. 88–89.

13 Ibid., p. 94.

14 'All About the Fast' by Gandhi, *Young India*, 25 September 1924; *Collected Works,* 25: 202.

15 *Bombay Chronicle,* 16 September 1927; *Collected Works,* 34: 538.

16 Remarks on 5 November 1917, to an Antyaj Conference, or a conference of the lowest-born, in Godhra, Gujarat. *Collected Works,* 14: 75.

17 16 February 1916, at students' meeting, YMCA, Madras, *Collected Works,* 13: 232.

18 Preface to *Antyaj Stotra*, Nadiad, 17 April 1918; *Collected Works,* 14: 345.

19 *Young India*, 11 October 1928; *Collected Works,* 37: 349.

20 Dictated remarks at prayer meeting, Delhi, 18 January 1948; *Collected Works,* 90: 452.

21 A. J. Parel (ed.), *Gandhi: Hind Swaraj*, New Delhi: Cambridge University Press, 1997, pp. 52–54.

22 M. K. Gandhi, *The Story of My Experiments with Truth,* Ahmedabad: Navajivan, 1927, vol. 1, p. 322.

23 *Indian Opinion*, 9 November 1907, *Collected Works,* 7: 510.

24 *Young India,* 1 June 1921; *Collected Works,* 20: 159.

25 *Young India*, 11 October 1928; *Collected Works,* 37: 339.

26 Edited quotation by Omar el-Haqqaq in B. R. Nanda (ed.), *Mahatma Gandhi: 125 Years*, New Delhi: Indian Council for Cultural Relations, 1995, p. 80.
27 *Collected Works*, 87: 182–83.
28 *Collected Works*, 87: 192–93.
29 *Collected Works,* 90: 61.
30 *Collected Works,* 89: 250.
31 *Collected Works,* 90: 18.
32 *Hind Swaraj*, p. 94.
33 Churchill's remark in the House of Commons, 12 March 1931. Quoted in Robert Rhodes James (ed.), *Winston Churchill: His Complete Speeches*, New York: Chelsea House, 1974, vol. V (1928–1935), p. 4995.
34 Speech at Karachi Congress session, 26 March 1931, *Collected Works,* 45: 349.
35 James M. Lawson Jr, *Revolutionary Nonviolence*, Oakland, CA: University of California Press, 2022, p. 79.
36 Remarks quoted in D. G. Tendulkar, *Abdul Ghaffar Khan: Faith Is a Battle*, Bombay: Popular Prakashan, pp. 264–65.
37 *Collected Works,* 90: 425.
38 *Harijan,* 10 November 1940; *Collected Works,* 73: 125-26.
39 PTI, '"No Need To Search For Temple Or Shivling Everywhere": RSS Chief Mohan Bhagwat', *NDTV.com*, 29 August 2025.

40 Speech of 16 September 1940 in *Harijan Sevak*, 12 October 1940; *Collected Works,* 79: 231.
41 V. P. Menon, *Transfer of Power*, Calcutta: Orient Longman, pp. 358–59.
42 Rajmohan Gandhi, *Patel: A Life*, Ahmedabad: Navajivan, 1991, pp. 385–88.
43 *Collected Works,* 87: 253–54.
44 *Collected Works,* 87: 257.
45 Entry dated 13 April 1947, Rajagopalachari Papers.
46 *Collected Works,* 88: 118.
47 Remarks to AICC, 14 June 1947, New Delhi, *Collected Works*, 88: 154.
48 B. N. Joj, *Threat of Islam*, Bombay: Unnati Prakashan, 1994, p. 466.
49 Muhammad Mujeeb, *Indian Muslims*, London: George Allen and Unwin Ltd, 1956, p. 233.
50 Amish, *Raavan*, New Delhi: HarperCollins India, 2019, pp. 3–4.
51 Robert Orme, *A History of the Military Transactions of the British Nation in Indostan, from the year MDCCXLV; to which is Prefixed a Dissertation on the Establishments made by Mahomedan conquerors in Indostan*, London: John Nourse, 1778. Reprinted, n.d., in New Delhi by Today's and Tomorrow's Printers and Publishers, vol. 2, p. 7.
52 R. C. Majumdar, *Ancient India*, Calcutta: University of

Calcutta, 1952, second edition, 1960, p. 347.

53 Chapter by Pusalker in R. C. Majumdar, General Editor, *History and Culture of the Indian People, Volume 01, 'The Vedic Age'*, Mumbai: Bharatiya Vidya Bhavan, 2017, p. 332.

54 Foreword by Munshi in Majumdar, *History and Culture of the Indian People*, p. 12.

55 Ibid., pp. 10–12.

56 '*Matru Bhumi*', a translation of the *Prithvi Sukta* in the Atharva Veda, by Harivallabh 'Hari', Ajmer: Archana Prakashan, 1980, available on archive.org

57 'How Tulsi Gabbard, the first Hindu-American US Director of National Intelligence, was introduced to Hinduism by her parents', *Times of India*, 16 November 2024.

58 'Religious Landscape Study', Pew Research Center, 26 February 2025.

59 'Religion in America: U.S. Religious Data, Demographics and Statistics', Pew Research Center.

60 'Hindu population change', *How the Global Religious Landscape Changed From 2010 to 2020*, Pew Research Center, 9 June 2025.

61 D. S. Sarma, *Renascent Hinduism*, Bombay: Bhavan, 1966, p. 130.

62 Francesca Regalado, '20 States Sue to Block $100,000 Fee for H-1B Visas', *New York Times*, 13 December 2025.

63 'WATCH: Trump signs order that adds $100K annual fee to H-1B visas for high-skilled workers', PBS.org, 20 September 2025.

64 '"Tariff Call Centres": US Influencers Target India Over Visas, Immigration', *NDTV.com*, 4 September 2025.

65 'Man Who Beheaded Indian National At US Motel Faces Deportation', *NDTV.com*, 13 September 2025.

66 'US Man Reacts To H-1B Visa, Says "I Want My Kids To Grow Up In America, Not India", Sparks Debate', *NDTV.com*, 7 September 2025.

67 'Over 100,000 attend London rally organized by far-right activist, clashes break out', *NPR*, 13 September 2025.

68 'Tommy Robinson Hails Modi As He Says Pakistan Is a Terror State, Time to Free Balochistan', CNN-News18.

69 'Country profiles list', Australian Government, Department of Home Affairs.

70 'Investigation finds links between white nationalist views and March for Australia organisers', ABC News, 28 August 2025.

71 Divya A, '"Everyone regardless of faith or heritage, has the right to feel safe": Australian Minister Anne Aly after anti-India protests', *Indian Express*, 19 October 2025.

72 '"JD Vance's Wife Isn't Muslim": Trump Ally's Shocker

To Journalist', *NDTV.com*, 26 October 2025.

73 Cauvery Madhavan, 'When I left India, Ireland welcomed me in. I won't let bigotry destroy the country we love', *The Guardian*, 8 September 2025.

74 Jim Geraghty, 'The RSS is a warning to all nations where populism is spiking', *Washington Post*, 14 October 2025.

75 Dheeraj Mishra, 'Lesson in hate: In Muzaffarnagar school, teacher gets kids to beat Muslim student, one by one', *Indian Express*, 30 August 2023; Meer Faisal, 'Outrage in India over video of teacher telling kids to slap Muslim student', *Aljazeera*, 25 August 2023.

76 M. K. Gandhi, *The Story of My Experiments with Truth*, vol. I, p. 359.

77 Moumita Alam, 'The Light That Peeps in Through the Holes: Two Poems on Rat-Hole Miners', *Livewire*, 1 December 2023.